STREET CREDO

Contributors

Given in order of publication

Michael Simmons, the general editor of *Street Credo*, is former Deputy Editor of the Society section of the Guardian, and has spent most of his journalistic career writing for quality British newspapers about social and economic developments in Britain and Europe. His previous books include *Landscapes- of Poverty; Berlin-the Dispossessed City; The Unloved Country; The Reluctant President: A political life of Vaclav Havel.*

Rev. Malcolm Brown is executive secretary of the William Temple Foundation, Manchester.

Rev. Andrew Mawson is Chairman of the Bromley by Bow Centre in London's East End and Co-Director of Community Action Network (CAN).

Simon Barrow is associate secretary of the Churches' Commission on Mission at Churches Together in Britain and Ireland. He teaches at the South-East Institute for Theological Education and was formerly the adult education and training officer for Southwark Anglican Diocese.

Dr Jim McDonnell is director of the Catholic Communications Centre, London.

Catherine Shelley was the first Parliamentary officer for Church Action on Poverty, editor of the *Christian Socialist* Magazine, and is now a labour councillor in Brighton and Hove.

Pauline Haughton is director of Kenté, a voluntary organisation which works with ethnic minority organisations in the London area.

Rev. Pen Wilcock is minister for Keston and West Wickham churches in the Bromley Methodist Circuit.

Rev. Peter Barham is based at Bury St Edmunds and is priest-in-charge at Bradfield St Clare, Cockfield, Felsham and Gedding.

Richard Lindley is director of education for the Winchester Diocese and was formerly director of education for the Birmingham Diocese.

Terry Drummond is adviser on social responsibility and industrial mission for the Croydon episcopal area is Chair of Community Health UK.

Denise Mumford is a retired social worker and former director of WelCare in Southwark Diocese, London.

Dr Patrick Logan is housing and homelessness adviser for the Diocese of Southwark.

Niall Cooper is national co-ordinator of Church Action on Poverty. He was formerly national organiser of the Churches National Housing Coalition.

Russell Webster is an independent consultant specialising in partnership approaches to dealing with substance misuse and crime.

Gerard Lemos is the co-author with Michael Young (Lord Young of Dartington) of The Communities We Have Lost and Can Regain.

Rev Giles Goddard is rector of St Peters, Walworth in London.

STREET CREDO

CHURCHES IN THE COMMUNITY

Edited by Michael Simmons

Lemos&Crane

First published in 2000 by
Lemos & Crane
20 Pond Square
Highgate
London N6 6BA

ISBN 1-898001-69-3

A CIP catalogue record for this book is
available from the British Library.

Cover design by Bluefrog Ltd, London
Printed and bound by Redwood Books Ltd, Trowbridge

Contents

Introduction
Bridging gaps
By Michael Simmons

At the start of the new Millennium, leaders of all religions occupy a potentially powerful position. They find themselves in that ill-defined space between demands of the policy-makers and the aspirations of the communities around them. But while some of them have been quick on their feet, have found ways of exercising their power and bridging the gap, others remain perplexed, daunted by, among other things, falling numbers of worshippers and increasing questions about the continuing validity of faith in a high pressure world.

This book does not set out to offer solutions, but it does seek to discuss common problems in a constructive way. It is not intended as a DIY manual on how to bridge gaps, but it does seek to examine critically the relevance of faith and, in some cases, what faith has achieved, in a series of complicated social environments. The contributors are people directly or indirectly connected to various Christian denominations in England with first hand experience of the areas about which they have written – but equally important, they have also sought to reflect on the impact that faith has had on their work in the wider community.

The pages that follow are not intended in any sense to be exclusive. How could they be when five important faiths are actively staking their claims to a place in multi-cultural Britain: Jews, Muslims, Hindus and Sikhs, as well as Christians? At a time when the policy-makers are trying to meet the needs of all sorts of minorities, to provide for those in all sorts of need, and to bring in from the cold those who feel disadvantaged or excluded, no religious leader can afford to proclaim his or her "way" is better than anyone else's way. They can only say "This is one way of bridging the gap."

The Government itself has openly acknowledged that faith groups of all religions may be the strongest community organisations in a given area, and also that their "potential" may still be overlooked by funders. A Home Office report of September 1999 conceded that "black majority churches, mosques, temples, gurudwaras are well represented in faith communities and are particularly strong in identifying and responding to unmet needs in black and minority ethnic communities."

In many areas in Britain, ethnic minority churches have seen their congregations, and their community role, growing. Where local or national policy makers have been unable, for whatever reason, to meet local needs, these churches have stepped in, making a difference in provision for children, for the elderly and the impoverished and in campaigning against race prejudice.

Hindu, Muslim and Sikh leaders have successfully developed activities that go far beyond the provision of facilities for worship. They have provided forums for discussion, and even measurable opportunities, in matters of education, employment and health, and where appropriate have looked after the culturally sensitive needs of women in their communities. It is in the interest of local and national policy-makers that these faith groups, like the many activities over which they preside, should not be ignored.

But despite all this, there is no denying the fact that the sense of order and social cohesiveness which many would claim was discernible in Britain and in countless other societies a century ago has gone. Frequently, it has been eroded by a process of social disintegration that seems in so many areas to have gained in momentum as the century progressed. Values which shaped communities have also changed out of all recognition as the communities themselves have faced unexpected competition for their attention and allegiance.

For more than two decades, as a working journalist, I was able to observe at first hand the social and economic developments that were taking place in the Communist-led countries of East Europe. I went, whenever I could, to visit remoter, smaller communities, asking local people, when I could gain their confidence, to share some of their "real" feelings. The response all too frequently was the same: there was little or no respect for "the authorities", there was little community coherence and viable leadership was conspicuously missing.

Then, from the early 1999s, I spent half a dozen years, reporting social and economic change in Britain. I talked to men and women in the inner cities and in deprived rural areas about their voting intentions, and about their attitudes to people in power. All too often, the response was an echo of the one I had heard in totalitarian Eastern Europe. It was spelled out in short, blunt sentences – sometimes quite colourful – concluded with a shrug of the shoulders before the speaker moved on.

Britain has embarked on the new century as a country of uncertain points of reference, where political terms of engagement have too often been determined by short-term considerations along party lines. At the same time, it is a country where leading political practitioners have sought to present themselves as conciliators, as men of freshly-minted faith – in this case, the Christian faith. It is the voters who have professed a certain political agnosticism, nursing suppressed but often justifiable reservations about the men and women they have elected into power. Scepticism and cynicism among the electorate have become endemic: the sleaze of one party, the argument runs, has been replaced by the cronyism of another.

Where religious leaders have had the resources of imagination, of personnel (however few), of buildings and of willpower to make things happen, they have been able to achieve great things in local terms. Furthermore, in sensitive and important areas of social concern, which impinge daily on the lives of communities, they have been involved, often to great effect. Arguments have been joined, sometimes with much relish.

In inviting the contributors to write, I left it to them to choose whether to write anecdotally or analytically about the implications, as they saw them, of their experience of their "areas". But I asked in each case that they should write with at least one eye on the religious perspective. This means some of the writers have concluded by asking questions, while others have felt about to suggest solutions, drawing on personal and/or community experience. Others, in wider areas of social concern, have constructed arguments. Solutions are not always easy.

If the writers have chosen to dip their toes, or more, into controversial waters, that has been a matter for them. We have quite consciously chosen not to present their words as contributions to a handbook on How to Deal with Crime, or How to Run a Church of England school, or whatever, but as a series of essays which will show the relevance and the resilience of religion in important areas of concern in everyday life.

The chosen themes are intended to reflect contemporary concerns. But, as the opening chapters indicate, there is an implicit challenge in defining terms and parameters. Malcolm Brown, drawing on teaching as well as preaching experience, seeks to meet that challenge, while in (uncharted) waters that are almost as deep, Andrew Mawson tells of the trials, tribulations and pleasures that he and others encountered when they set about creating a community almost from scratch in London's East End.

What might be called the eternal role of the Church – that of guide, philosopher and friend – remains paramount, and is explored here by Simon Barrow. The Internet has a place, too, and communication of a different, contemporary sort is covered by Jim McDonnell. But disadvantage and unemployment are among the imperatives of the age, as Catherine Shelley and Paulette Haughton underline.

Experiences of the community *in situ* vary according to context – which is why there are separate chapters on the suburban experience (Pen Wilcock) and the rural one (Peter Barham). Then, in the broader sense of community, there is the Church as a catalyst in areas of activity such as education (Richard Lindley) and health (Terry Drummond).

Finally, and all-importantly, there are specific issues that concern the Church – professionals and lay people equally – which are the stuff of daily headlines. Denise Mumford discusses how the role of women has changed, specifically in the last century. Patrick Logan tackles the perennially thorny issues of asylum seekers. Niall Cooper, active until very recently in the churches' own housing coalition, talks about homelessness as a housing issue. Finally, Russell Webster, drawing on work done in inner-city London and elsewhere, looks at where the Church fits into the debates about crime.

In every chapter, the views expressed are those of the individual writers themselves and not, unless stated, of the organisations of which they may be part.

Readers may wish to know that the book itself came about after a number of very helpful discussions between myself and some senior luminaries of the Church Urban Fund. I am especially grateful for the exchanges I had at an early stage with Angela Sarkis, CUF's somewhat redoubtable chief executive. But acknowledgements and thanks are due not only to CUF but also to other organisations and individuals – most conspicuously, to Giles Goddard – who all made encouraging noises or expressed constructive reservations along the way to publication.

Michael Simmons, the general editor of *Street Credo*, is former Deputy Editor of the Society section of the *Guardian*.

Chapter One

God's image:
Whose Church?
Which Community?

By Malcolm Brown

Meanings can be slippery. Few words carry so many vague and contradictory meanings as "church" and "community", yet both bear within them concepts that are central to an understanding of social history and to an analysis of how we live now. They are important words because the ideas they convey are critical to human flourishing. But they are also words that are rarely very far from conflict. The amount of blood spilt through the centuries over the idea of "church" is notorious and, as secularisation leeches away the passion from "holy wars", rival notions of community seem poised to take their place as a focus for intransigent opposition.

Imagine you are the picture editor illustrating the theme of "Churches and Community". What images would you choose? Perhaps an urban scene, maybe a rather rundown but lively street. You would hardly choose a view of suburbia where all the symbols – the hedges, the garden gates, the ostentatious privacy – speak of social atomism, of "keeping ourselves to ourselves". But you might go for a picture of a rural village – in many ways the archetypal community. Here, it seems, the lives of people are focused on common experiences, and even a highly stratified, class-dominated structure is brought together in some understanding of local identity.

That, at least, is the theory. And that is why the village is so often the starting point for the Church's image of itself within community. In the idealised village, the church takes its place alongside the pub, the post office and the school as the public expression of local identity. Indeed, as probably the oldest and most architecturally distinctive building in the place, the church may perhaps be the supreme symbol of rural community identity.

The village church, of flint or stone, doubtless endures. The post office, school and often the pub have frequently gone the way of the rural branchline and bus service. And while the church building may remain unchanged, the worshipping life it now represents would probably be unrecognisable to our rural forebears. The sight of a country church, with the lane outside blocked by the parked cars of worshippers, gives a somewhat ambiguous message about the church's relation to the community. Whose church? Which community?

So back to the urban imagery. Can we depict "community" best by showing homes or public space? Or is it civic identity – the library, the town hall – that represents "community" to the people? Or is it the great institutions of shared experience – the hospital, the school? Should our street scene be empty, perhaps to highlight the contradictory reality of "care in the community" for so many? Or should it be teeming with life? And if so, should the faces be smiling or drawn? In other words, what place is there for tension and difference in our idealised picture of community?

And how would we include the church in our urban picture? As a dark, Victorian example of social domination, a stranded whale of a building whose intended context has been lost? Or a modern church with its subtly defensive architecture, designed to be secure from the implicit violence of urban life? (Which group's social analysis underpins the design of churches is a fascinating line of inquiry).

The fact is that we can use our illustration to establish several distinctive – and not necessarily compatible – perspectives on "church" and on "community". Every picture will be contentious. None will convey a full richness of meaning. Each will mislead in one direction or another. But the illustrations we may select reflect the pictures in our heads. It is possible to build up wide-ranging coalitions around the ideas of church and community, but when the images begin to become specific, the extent of agreement and ability to work together may be much less than imagined.

I begin in this vein because I believe that the Christian churches in England (my experience is of England, although my knowledge of other parts of Britain and Europe suggests similar patterns) are at something of a crisis point about their own identity. What is at issue is the nature of the church as a community and within a community. And until some new settlement has been reached, talk of church and community risks becoming the proverbial dialogue of the deaf as rival and incommensurable images of both church and community jostle for ascendancy.

This is where the myth of rural community emerges as a powerful influence in contemporary thinking. The coincidence of parish boundaries defining an area of "civil space" and an area of ecclesiastical jurisdiction is no accident; it is a relic of a historic inseparability of church and community, long pre-dating Anglicanism. It is all part of the powerful myth of all life being lived under the benevolent wing of Mother Church – indeed, of the ordering of the whole of existence within a Christian world-view and vocabulary. Like all powerful myths, it has roots in truth (though not the whole truth) and has considerable formative influence on present thought. It leaves us with an instinctive sense that the church (as the people of God) and the community (as the people of the place) are essentially the same thing.

If it were ever so, it is so no longer. It is not necessary to go into a detailed account of secularisation, plurality and multi-culturalism. These concepts are disputed both as historical processes and as definitions of our present state. But the fact remains that they are words which attempt to describe a reality that cannot be escaped. The conflation of culture with Christendom has long been unsustainable. And this is perhaps a situation that Anglicans have yet to perceive with quite the acuteness that the dissenting Christian traditions recognise.

One consequence is that the churches have had to become more self-conscious of their own nature as communities. As the division between sacred and secular has opened up, and as people's lives have become more consciously compartmentalised, belonging to the church in its local, national and global manifestations has become something which requires a conscious choice. And as religion of any kind is now understood culturally as optional (in that most people seem to get along fine without overt religious allegiances), to belong to a "faith community" is to stand out, at some level, against the prevailing culture.

Yet rarely, if ever, does Christian or any other religious faith entail separation from mainstream culture. We become members of many communities and, within ourselves, negotiate the tensions and contradictions between them. The values, behavioural norms and vocabularies of neighbourhood, class, work, gender, religion and so on, weave complex patterns throughout our lives. In each form of belonging it can be said that we inhabit a community. Faith communities may still speak among themselves as if their religion offered a grand narrative for the whole of existence, but the reality is that faith takes its place, at certain times and places, alongside many other discourses.

If the foregoing has laboured the point it is only because the role of the churches within a plural culture is so often misunderstood – and not only by the churches. A few years ago I did some research into the role of churches in arms conversion and diversification projects and met several secular groupings working in this field who actively sought partnerships with local churches in the belief that this would give them a dialogue with "the community". The same assumptions recur now that the concept of partnership is so often the mantra which replaces old notions of public, private and voluntary provision in so many fields. Churches are in danger of being flattered into believing that they can in some way speak for, or deliver, "the community". The old models of Christendom are an unconscionable time a-dying, and the risk of inadvertent collusion between churches and powerful vested interests is acute.

It is worth noting, at this point, that the social plurality which constitutes today's context is both a product and a consequence of the dominance of free market ideologies which extend well beyond the traditional domain of the economist. This is not simply the old game of "blame Thatcherism for the state we're in", but a matter of taking the market seriously on its own terms. Fundamentally, the market offers itself as a response to social and ethical plurality. The fact that Margaret Thatcher's governments combined market liberalism with authoritarian conservative social policies tended to obscure the manner in which market economics presumes that there is no widespread social consensus by which distributional justice can be agreed. Attempts to direct the economy towards socially-just outcomes were seen as no less than coercion of the majority by a self-styled intellectual elite.

These are the philosophical roots of Thatcherism's antipathy to "community" – at least, to appeals to "community" as a virtue which stood in the way of deregulated market outcomes. And, fascinatingly, the gurus of the New Right had caught an echo of an important critique from the Left: that many social institutions used the vocabulary of "community", "public" and "common good" to obscure the sectional vested interests of the people (doctors, teachers, government officers) who ran those institutions. In other words, left and right understood that, in a plural society with no unifying story about belonging, public virtue was too often a front for private pleading. It was the genius of Thatcherism to turn this into an all-embracing ideological and economic critique.

It often feels as if those in the churches and elsewhere who opposed the Thatcher project so volubly failed to understand the moral force of the New Right arguments. In the wake of *Faith in the City* (1985), Prof. Raymond Plant spent a great deal of time acting as devil's advocate in order to stir the churches to a more profound engagement and critique of Thatcherism. As Plant pointed out, appeals to the virtues of community not only fell on deaf ears, they were too often devoid of content. A. H. Halsey had written in 1974 that community "has so many meanings as to be meaningless", and Plant went on to argue that the word was too often simply an expression of nostalgic warmth, and that community values themselves had often been forged in the reaction to massive societal upheavals.

So how can the virtues denoted by the word "community" be given more concrete substance? It's interesting to remember that Thatcher and Co. were actually quite comfortable with the idea of community, so long as it meant no more than the kind of associations which people choose to join. They had no problem with churches, scout groups or even pressure groups, provided that they spoke only for their paid-up members and never presumed to articulate any wider interest. But the idea that a complex web of relationships – an organic interplay of diverse interests – might constitute something called "community" was anathema to the mentality of market individualism.

This brief excursion into the recent past may seem like ancient history. The New Labour government elected in May 1997 has done a good deal to open up the boundaries of what may be debated. This makes it depressing to read a pamphlet on *Civic Spirit* published by Demos and find little in it from which a

Thatcherite would dissent. The model of social relationships offered here is that of the voluntary "club". The author recognises that such bodies can be inward-looking, exclusive, racist, and so on. Indeed they can, and Demos offers us no guidance on how such traits can be avoided.

This is certainly a very thin model of community. But the ability of the churches to pursue a broader vision is limited by their own nervousness about their place in society, and the perception – often accurate – that churches function very like elective clubs for people who like that sort of thing. The challenge now is to create something more true to human experience, which is richer than the "market model" but which avoids the authoritarian imposition of a single narrative of community that fits too few lives.

Despite the unprecedented impact of *Faith in the City* and similar work by other denominations, the trend in the 1990s has been for the churches to become embroiled in matters of internal maintenance, to the detriment of their engagement with, and mission among, the structures and institutions that shape the day to day lives of people – Christian or otherwise. It is as if the churches, having begun to understand their marginal position in a post-Christendom secular society, have swallowed the market ideology which had no place for community beyond the associational club. The false dichotomy of this thinking (unified, consensual society versus market individualism; the grand narrative of Christianity or atomised moral relativism) has done much harm. There are resources in Christian theology for the Church, as the community of the faithful, to play a full part in a vibrant wider community in ways that are respectful of difference, conscious of the ambiguity of power and committed to transformative social action. I will return to this vision, but meanwhile it is necessary to look more deeply at why theological understandings of the church within civil society are currently so neglected or disparaged.

Thinking back to the reaction to *Faith in the City* in the mid-1980s, it has become clear that accusations of theological inadequacy made about the report at the time were at least partly justified. *Faith in the City* was the report of a Commission conceived on the principle of a panel of "experts" examining the "facts" and reporting – first to the Church of England, but secondly, and with all the confident assumptions of an established church, to government. Yet, theologically, the report flirted strongly with the partisan, perspectival, concepts of Liberation Theology – theology conceived by the marginalised and eschewing liberal notions of balance, objectivity and inclusiveness. Liberation Theology gave *Faith in the City* its passion and its disturbing power. But if it was liberationist in tone, the structure and methods of the Commission itself – and, even more, the structures and tendencies of the church to which it was addressed – pulled in the opposite direction. *Faith in the City* embodied the tensions within a church still wedded to being an "estate of the realm" but increasingly marginal within a society that was itself fracturing, marginalising whole communities in a material and tangible sense, as the consensus around welfare economics crumbled.

In this plural context, where assumptions about the dominance of the Christian narrative are manifestly challenged by new perceptions of diversity and particularity, the Christian community has, not surprisingly, been forced to examine its own identity. What distinguishes Christian faith from varieties of secular culture? In what ways is the community of the faithful distinctive within the plethora of communities competing for their social interests?

The focus on Christian identity is timely and necessary. It is therefore depressing that major contemporary trends in Christian social ethics stress the matter of distinctiveness in ways that preclude mutually respectful dialogue with other traditions and narratives. Instead, the emphasis – either overtly or implicitly – is triumphalist. A key figure here is the American theologian Stanley Hauerwas, for whom the character of the Christian community is essentially counter-cultural. The calling of the Church is to live as if the Kingdom of God were fully present among us and to reflect in its own life the gospel values characteristic of the heavenly community. There is little here about the messy business of being simultaneously a citizen of earthly kingdoms and incommensurable, overlapping communities. In Britain, Hauerwas's position is amplified by theologians like Michael Banner who are frankly contemptuous of "liberal"theologies which attempt to restate Christian truth in terms amenable to secular sociology. The treatment of "experience" as the benchmark against which theological analysis is to be measured is rejected in favour of a re-emphasis of God's revelation of His ultimate truths. From different theological roots, John Milbank's work attempts to fashion a Christian grand narrative that will "out-narrate" rival, inferior narratives – especially the dominant Enlightenment discourse of "secular reason".

What characterises these theologians is an emphatic certainty about the finality and truth of the revelation of God in Christ and the character of the Church as the community which embodies those truths, living them out for the conversion of the world. In the face of the self-confidence – some would say stridency – of these theologies, the old ascendancy of liberalism within the churches, and its characteristic methodology of respectful dialogue with secular disciplines (and, thus, with wider communities), is in marked retreat. The loss of confidence is tangible.

It may be argued that the introspections of academic theologians have little effect on the practice of the local church, embedded for better or worse in the context of its wider community. But when the mood music in academe changes it is not long before the tune is being whistled on the streets. The resurgence of a theological emphasis on the distinctiveness and uniqueness of the church as a community – as the exemplary community – coincides with the political reality of a church which is tired of the complexities of politics, confused by the fragmentation of society and fearful of its own potential for rancorous division. A theological fig-leaf (though the theologians mentioned are much more than this) to cover the Church's social insecurity is there to avoid ecclesiastical embarrassment.

But in these struggles the churches are not alone. Just as theologies of distinctiveness imply firm boundaries to the community of faith, so the collapse of unifying stories about nationhood, citizenship and community are leading to more confrontational politics on the ground among activists – including those from the churches or motivated by faith. Here the stories of community development and community organising (both of which need to be told at much greater length) are significant.

What might be called "traditional" community development work might once have been described as the radical cutting-edge of the churches' social engagement. The "working with, not for" principle enshrined the notion of empowerment and the fundamental belief in the innate capacity of hard-pressed people to discover within themselves the resources for their liberation – or, at least, for the marginal improvement of their lives. There is a vital theological resonance here with the idea of the God who is present in all his creation, who "gets there before we do" and shines in the lives of people who do not acknowledge Him.

Expressed like this, it is clear that community development work is likely to have a rather low view of the significance of the Church, and probably a rather minimal view of the distinctive nature of Christian belief. Not surprisingly, then, community development work has found itself (along with Industrial Mission, Social Responsibility and the other established agencies of church engagement with the secular) at the decidedly unfashionable end of the theological spectrum. Liberals within the churches who, while priding themselves on their perceived radicalism, always portrayed themselves as a minority within the institutional church now find themselves derided as part of a decaying liberal ascendancy that has been in power too long. For the new radicals in theology, the search for social relevance is as great a chimera as the pursuit of social justice was to the New Right economists.

Nor can community workers point to sufficient practical outcomes to endear themselves on the grounds of effectiveness. "Making a difference" to people's lives is often achieved in small ways, unknown to the principal workers concerned. The tiny thing that forges relationships in the community and may make life marginally more endurable is an outcome in a different league from the measurable differences demanded by funders – church and otherwise. Drawn inexorably into the numbers game and pressured for unachievable results by well-meaning supporters longing for an end to poverty and misery (and by less well-meaning "principalities and power" driven by accountancy values and "innovation" at all costs), it is hardly surprising that community development is in the doldrums. Its undoubted virtues – respect for difference, trust in reason, the belief in a God bigger than the Church – are out of kilter with the spirit of the age. And it has to be said that, in terms both of theological coherence and social analysis, community development has, with many other fields, been in need of new ideas and energies for some time.

More strident and self-confident, the community organising movement (often known as Broad Based Organising) is a highly significant phenomenon. Churches and other faith communities have often been enthusiastic partners in this movement, which seeks to create large-scale coalitions among the people of a neighbourhood in order to take up contentious local issues and confront those in power with their demands. A central figure is the organiser, trained in the methods associated originally with Saul Alinsky's work in Chicago, and often not themselves a local person. The disparagement of community development methods within the community organising movement recalls the fervour of converts (which many are) and, like some of the new strands in theology, dwells on the rightness of a particular community's perspective and a refusal to temporise with rival understandings.

In this, and in its profoundly pragmatic analysis of power relations, community organising is very much of the times – or at least of the market-driven, utilitarian politics of the 1980s and early 1990s. "To the strong, the spoils" might be the motto, and the objective is to realise the latent strength of communities marginalised and weakened by their inability to organise. It is not difficult to see the theological attractiveness to the churches of a movement in which the armies of good and evil are so plainly delineated and where the opportunity to "choose the good" (and, incidentally, to submerge the self) is so openly offered.

But if community organising is a movement of the times, it also displays the weaknesses of the dominant social and theological analysis. In brief, it seems too quickly dismissive of the complexities and ambiguities both of power and of the nature of community. The identification of "opponents" and the focus on "winnable actions" sits ill with theological perceptions of humanity's "solidarity in sin" and the paradoxical nature of victory which – both on the cross and in everyday life – tends to emerge in unexpected ways. More pragmatically, it must be said that the exclusivity of the community organising movement, and its unwillingness to engage in dialogue where it is not in control of the terms of debate (and often an aversion to anything deemed to be "liberal"), has lost the movement some good opportunities to share elements of its method.

It cannot be denied, though, that movements such as this force us to re-examine what we mean by "community". If the

Right was correct in limiting "community" to voluntary associations, then the logical extension of that idea is for small associations to combine around shared issues. At one level, the community organising movement is replaying the history of the trade union movement by countering the power of wealth and influence with the massed power of a disciplined, organised "proletariat". But, just as the trade unions now service an increasingly middle-class membership and are poorly represented among the marginal workforce, so there appears to be nothing in the model to prevent community organising techniques from being taken up to defend the privileges of the relatively powerful against the interests of the weak.

This lack of an adequate analysis of power has sometimes been evident in other forms of community work too. To offer a personal example: in my first parish, in well-heeled Kent, we had community associations who were "part of the problem". Their prime function appeared to be to maintain the white barriers across the roads into their private estates and to force recalcitrant neighbours to mow their lawns at the required intervals. When I moved to a UPA parish in Southampton I found other community associations campaigning to get the lifts working in their tower blocks. Both used the emotive idea of community to validate their very different (and, I believe, morally different) objectives.

My point is that definitions of community alone give us no tools to distinguish these two groups. An analysis of power and a critique of ideology are essential to any critical, informed engagement by churches or others in communities. Many community activists in the churches have been much influenced by Liberation Theology and the associated method of theological reflection known as the Pastoral Cycle. Yet in the vast majority of cases where the Pastoral Cycle has been used in a European context, the vital step of Ideological Suspicion (examining and questioning the influence of unconsciously absorbed ideology on those using the Cycle) has been omitted or treated perfunctorily. This, I suspect, may be a particularly dangerous omission in the current climate of enthusiasm for public, private and voluntary sector partnership approaches to economic regeneration and welfare provision. Not only are the churches at risk, yet again, of being regarded as representative of the community, but the danger of cosy alliances between articulate, comfortable professionals stitching up deals that affect the voiceless and marginalised may go unchallenged. Churches, and church representatives, drawn into these partnership projects would do well to remember Tony Benn's five questions to people with power: What power do you have? Who gave you that power? On whose behalf do you use that power? To whom are you accountable? How can we get rid of you? To paraphrase the baptism service, we must answer these questions for ourselves and for those others.

An adequate understanding of power is an important antidote to the tendency to treat every claim to be a community as equally valid. It is also an important factor in challenging the central assumption of market economics that what matters is the moral validity of the process (the market itself), not the distributional outcomes which exacerbate the gulf of wealth and power between rich and poor. It has long been established that market economics not only presumes the absence of a moral consensus but actively erodes the shared moral fabric on which market and non-market aspects of life alike depend.

One very tangible aspect of this is the flexible labour market. The impact of new patterns of work on community life are, perhaps, only just beginning to be understood. When, in the mid-1990s, my own organisation reviewed its community-education project work it was to find that, where we had once been working predominantly with unemployed or unwaged people, the demands of part-time, casual and temporary work in various forms now presented immense barriers to people's participation in community-building activities. Nor did this involvement in the labour force bring new wealth into the area; on balance, most people were no better off than on benefit. New government policies on Welfare to Work and the Minimum Wage may ease that situation, but as "flexible" patterns of work take over new areas of the labour market the effect on community work and volunteering will only deepen.

The last 10 years have seen the loss of the concept of common time – the pattern where most people's working and leisure times coincided. The "24-hour society" is, in fact, the 24-hour market place. No longer can the nurture of community take place in shared time, largely uninvaded by market values. For the churches, the erosion of common time is an acute, but largely unnoticed, problem. My colleague, Alison Peacock, researching the impact of "flexible" work on church life, points to the increasing economic activity of women, the expansion of part-time working, weekend, shift and night-working as important factors in declining rates of church attendance. And these changes do not conform to old categories.

Congregational studies based on taxonomies of class, gender, education and affluence are in danger of missing highly significant trends. Peacock asks: "How may the churches reaffirm and express in practical action a sense of inclusive community in an employment context which appears to deny the need for 'shared recreation as a part of the basis of society'?" In this, significantly, the churches are in the same boat as other communities and groupings. Theological distinctiveness alone is unlikely to point ways forward when the presenting problem is that church members are constrained by their membership of wider economic communities. The theological resources that might help are those which might also address the baleful influences of the market on civil society and which work with a paradigm of the Christian community as one distinctive sort of belonging within the complex set of overlapping communities which people inhabit.

Theologically, the best hope for the church as a community may lie in a richer perception of what community might be. Following the moral philosopher Alasdair MacIntyre (who calls for new forms of community to preserve the virtues of civil society through the "new dark ages" that are already upon us), we can understand communities better through exploring the related ideas of tradition, narrative and character. Communities, then, are not just coalitions of interest groups but of people who share a story by which they try to live their lives – a story or stories about who they are, how they came to be there and whose side they take. The rich fabric of such narratives can come to constitute a tradition, and it is tradition that shapes the character of members of that community, setting out the virtues and values of what it means to be a good or true member. Community on these terms is organic, multi-layered and impossible to capture with the map of the planner or the bottom line of the accountant.

Left there, community could be a static and reactionary concept, but dynamism comes from the encounter between traditions and narratives in which new stories are generated and traditions learn from each other. Bodies like the (government-sponsored) Inner Cities Religious Council are important models, since the agendas of identity, difference and co-operation are focused on action for change in disadvantaged communities. Church groups who find themselves drawn into other partnerships for economic regeneration have sometimes done much to influence the world-view with which the partnership approaches its tasks – not least in holding to models of empowerment and participation understood theologically. So questions of authentic Christian identity are central. (One colleague, involved in inter-faith approaches to regeneration says, "The more I do this work, the more I become the Evangelical Christian I started out as: people need to know that I am clear about what I believe.") But a theology of engagement has to be there too. This implies openness to dialogue and a respect for difference and diversity, but also takes us back to the essential matter of power and its unequal distribution.

Christian theology, when it eschews triumphalism, is a real resource for encounter between communities. Conscious of the richness of its own narrative foundations – and of the tensions of interpretation that surround them – the Church should be able to recognise itself as more than an asssociational community. Because the Church has, historically, flourished most effectively within liberal democracies and in the context of a lively civil society, it should be the kind of community which works to secure and nourish the institutions of democracy and plurality. The introspective Church, on the other hand, jealous of its own purity, depends on wider communal structures which it does nothing to support. And the nature of the central narratives of Christianity – the story of salvation through the cross and resurrection – equip the Christian community with an acute (but paradoxical and therefore non-ideological) analysis of power.

The theologian Andrew Shanks sums up the calling of the Christian community in terms of three virtues: sanctity (which involves being true to the story of the community; transgression (which means a willingness to break boundaries and be changed by encounter with other traditions); and the "solidarity of the shaken" (which finds common ground with those whose lives have been disturbed by the social and economic context in which they are lived). But, Shanks adds, the churches will have difficulty with these virtues because it is trapped in a "pastoral monoculture" rooted in its self-perception as a persecuted community, "rather like someone who suffered abuse in infancy and has never fully recovered."

The churches need to focus again on a theology of the Interim – the period between Pentecost and the end of all things, in which we live with the presence of God among us but also with the persistence of sin; in which the Kingdom of God has been inaugurated but not yet realised. The new emphasis in theology which urges the Church to reflect the Kingdom reminds Christians of their calling. But, without the moderating influence of Christian Realism, the pursuit of an unworldly Kingdom risks closing down the engagement of the Church with the communities within which it is set. Because its members live between many communities, the unengaged Church fails their needs. And because the unengaged Church believes itself to be the possessor of God's final revelation, it may cease to learn from the God encountered beyond the Church.

The hope for the Church as a community among communities lies in its recognition that plurality and difference are not to be feared – because they are of God. In secular terms, communitarians who adopt authoritarian responses to "social deviancy" need to heed the same principle. As Harvey Cox noted in *The Secular City* (1965), we have outgrown the unified stories about ourselves which the rural myth generated. That maturing is to the good, but Cox was naive about power, about the way the logic of liberal relativism led to the market, and about the capacity of the consequent inequalities to distort the new community. Building community must now be about the solidarity of shaken people, conscious of the stories that give them identity, yet prepared to risk real encounters with people perceived as "other".

So which picture will we use to illustrate Church and community? It will be an urban scene, because there we stand a chance of escaping stultifying myths. It will include shops or traders, because the market is a large part of the context which both shapes and is challenged by community. There will, of course, be people, and they will embody between them much diversity; no community now lives by one story. And there will be some symbol of mediation, debate, dialogue – perhaps capturing a moment of confrontation or argument. Somewhere there will be an indication of the inequalities of power and wealth which loom over the lives of so many – it could be an intrusive, anonymous, post-modern office block, or a grille-protected police van. The church will be there, neither dominating the scene nor an irrelevance; the church building is only the outward sign of this community-within-communities and somehow we would need to show that it was for the people in the scene – a part of the fabric of their lives, but laying no oppressive claim on them all.

Capturing all that may be beyond the ingenuity of the photographer. But I can think of a few places where not only the images but the reality can be discovered most days of the week.

The **Rev. Malcolm Brown** is executive secretary of the William Temple Foundation, Manchester.

Chapter Two

The Pauline approach: Social entrepreneurs

by Andrew Mawson

One thing I like about living and working in East London is the native wit of its people against a background of considerable adversity. They have an ability to see the funnier side of life that always puts our human endeavours in perspective.

At a major ecumenical service in East London some time ago, I recall my organist describing how, during The Peace, she was approached by an over-zealous Christian, who grasped her hand and said: "May the sun shine up your garden path." "How else could I respond?" said Jenny, "but with the words, 'And up yours!'"

A while ago, I was asked by my moderator to describe, in a sentence, what had taken place over the last 14 years or so in Bromley by Bow to produce such a change. Just one sentence to tell her how a derelict church with 12 members now finds itself, 14 years on, employing 80 staff; running a budget in excess of £2 million per annum; dealing with over 2,000 people a week passing through the buildings; undergoing a £6 million development that will bring together, for the first time in the UK, a church, the arts, education projects, and will include the re-development of a three-acre park, 17 units of housing for homeless people, a new £1.5 million health centre, and 125 different activities taking place each week in an integrated project described as the first Healthy Living Centre in Britain and which was opened by the Minister for Public Health in March 1998.

At a church meeting we attempted to come up with some clever phrase which captured the reality of our experience. After we had struggled long and hard, and failed, Jenny suddenly piped up: "It's obvious what's happened here. When you came in 1984 we threw our knickers over the garden fence!"

We all realised that Jenny had captured in a sentence the risk-taking – both personally and as a community – we had been willing to undertake in order to challenge the prevailing apathy and bureaucratic log jams that prevent real change.

Four miles east of the City of London sits Bromley by Bow, an ancient community mentioned by Chaucer, once at the heart of the industrial revolution, but now a forgotten corner at the extreme eastern edge of the borough of Tower Hamlets. The 1991 government Index of Local Conditions ranked Tower Hamlets first in intensity of deprivation and second in extent of deprivation of any local authority in the country.

Bromley Ward has the second highest indices of deprivation in East London (19.06 against an East London average of 9.78), but has had very little investment (some derelict sites date back to the Second World War), being situated outside the various government initiatives, such as City Challenge.

The area demonstrates many of the worst aspects of urban decay, with poor health (16.3 per cent of residents have long-term illness), poor housing (up to 90 per cent rented) and low academic achievement (only 18 per cent get four GCSEs or more). It is an area of high population density, high levels of unemployment (males, 31.5 per cent; ethnic minorities, 47.3 per cent), and a diverse ethnic minority population (36 per cent ethnic minorities). Bordered by two major highways, it is disconnected from adjacent areas, which contributes to problems of isolation and the need for a community focus.

Despite all these difficulties, the area also houses a wealth of talent and opportunities – in part, as a result of the extraordinary diversity. However, this potential is not being realised. The City, foremost employer in the capital, is less than 15 minutes away, but could be 15 hours away for all the impact it had at that time.

The centre began at a time when the sparse and elderly church congregation agreed to offer their under-used buildings to the community. A number of artists living in the area became involved, giving classes to local people in return for using the workshop space rent-free. Others followed their example and soon a nursery, cafe, dance school and disability groups were set up, being run to the mutual benefit both of individuals and the wider community.

Since then we have sought to create a community space in which the entrepreneurial potential and creativity of local people can be explored. Projects have evolved around the five pillars of health, education, the arts, environment and enterprise. The centre has grown to include community care services, community education activities, art projects, ethnic minority programmes, health projects and urban regeneration schemes. Phase one of the redevelopment of a derelict park site adjacent to our buildings has been completed and a £1.5 million initiative to build a new GP and primary care centre was begun in February 1996. This is the first integrated community health facility of its kind in the country with the distinction of being owned directly by local people through a development trust – and with GPs paying rent to the patients!

The church at Bromley by Bow Centre stands at the heart of the project, both physically and spiritually. Our distinctive model of community development has grown from a theology that has sought to interpret the role of the church in the light of the complexity of the inner city and has tried to embrace that complexity without sentimentality or ideological compartmentalising. The liturgical space has been redesigned and remains a core sanctuary around which the bustle of the day revolves. Like the medieval cathedral, the church sits amid the market place of everyday activity, allowing the vibrancy and diversity of life to surround it and enabling a mutual crossover of influence between the secular and the sacred.

Our community development model is underpinned by the core values of creativity, excellence, integration and pragmatism. Our aim is to create effective social change within a framework of local, private and public sector partnership, leading to a community of confident individuals who are in a position to engage with the issues and bring about their own transformations.

It is an approach which is borne out of the recognition that traditional models of community development have generally failed the inner city and that the church – either working in isolation from the rest of the world, or hand in glove with the structures – has failed to be the carrier of effective transformation. We have based community development programmes on the pragmatic necessity for generating change that brings real improvement to the lives of individuals. It is, therefore, a model that is constantly changing. Like the gospel message itself, our approach can seem at times contradictory, but there are some core, underpinning values that are transferable to other contexts.

Based on our experience at Bromley by Bow, I believe there are 10 key propositions which need to become the mark of a Third Millennium Church if it is to share the treasures of Christian faith within the changing cultural, social and political landscape we all now inhabit, and within which politicians are struggling to find a footing.

1. A Third Millennium Church is about people, not structures

The Bromley by Bow Centre has grown around the charismatic energy of individuals, rather than structures or systems. We have embraced the concept of social entrepreneurs, encouraging individuals to run with their ideas and creating enough flexibility to allow people to experiment. We have set the benchmark of success as those ideas that lead to effective change. This is a community marked by a huge social deficit, and key staff are therefore charged with the task of being entrepreneurial in their work – creating social capital among the groups they work with. In this respect they are employed not to manage projects but to create environments which will encourage a sense of vision and motivation.

People themselves are the bricks of any sustainable regeneration process, and it is our belief that community growth is dependent upon creating the opportunities for individual growth. We have therefore adopted an approach that trains local people to become social entrepreneurs, strengthening the potential of individuals to make good things happen for themselves. It is a process that begins amid the details of people's lives and is dependent on the personal relationships that have grown between staff and local people over a number of years. We have dispensed with any sentimentality about the nature of democracy and the need for everyone to be involved in every decision. Instead, we have tried to build partnerships based on mutuality and friendship, recognising that trust between partners is essential if power and knowledge are to be used most effectively.

We have consciously avoided a model of community development that is based on consultation, meetings and forums. It is clear that these structures are familiar tools only to certain individuals – usually from outside our community – and that often minutes and meetings serve only to disempower local people further. The majority of people in this community do not run their lives around pieces of paper but are more likely to communicate through conversations and the process of engaging in each other's lives. It is therefore at this point that our process of consultation begins.

2. A Third Millennium Church must be about burying the dinosaurs of inflexibility and creating new frameworks for operation

The need to create structures which recognise the complexities of people's lives has led us to create a method of operation that is loose enough to allow people the freedom either to be proactive or to respond quickly to ideas, but tight enough to offer a framework of values which contribute to an overall sense of direction.

Our organisational structures have been set up with the absence of policies that define what is acceptable or unacceptable. The reality of people's lives on our estates is too complex to legislate around ideology or policies and so, for instance, we don't exclude people from the project for racism or sexism. There is instead a recognition that the language of the street does not always have the abusive meaning interpreted by the politically correct. And even when it is abusive, the context is generally too complicated to be resolved simply by a policy of exclusion. We have found that excluding people or views simply denies the complexities of the issues. It leads to an unhealthy environment in which everyone has the same views and in which the tensions arising from our diversity are lost as creative opportunities. Instead, we have sought to find the points of common ground amid our differences, recognising that there is more than one view in the world and that moving forward is dependent on making the connections between people, not severing the links.

The reality of life in the inner city is one of messiness. A sense of insecurity and the inability to plan or commit to anything regular is a prevalent pattern of existence for many people. We have therefore tried to create points of rhythm and regularity to the week around which people can focus their lives – for example, the Sunday liturgy, community cafe or gardening projects.

Similarly, we have found that the only way to enable people to participate in wider opportunities is to be extremely flexible in the provision of services. For example, we have structured our NVQ care training course around the details of people's lives, rather than around our organisational needs. This has led to a pattern of training that is extremely flexible and individualised, ensuring that courses are accessible to those who most need them. Ironically, this has prevented us from accessing the usual sources of training funding because achieving strict output measures are impossible, given the complications of people's lives. It is an approach which calls into question the structures set up to support community-based training – for instance, via TECs – and has forced us to look at finding alternative methods of evaluating the impact of community development programmes.

3. A Third Millennium Church must embrace a broader concept of ecumenism

The literal meaning of ecumenism – "the whole inhabited earth" – is what the Church must address. The endless dialogue between the churches is over; they must continue to turn outwards and engage with their local communities. The renewal of the Church and the renewal of our local communities are bound up together. The Bromley by Bow experience has demonstrated just how much we have to gain from each other if we can together discover the common ground we all share.

4. A Third Millennium Church must be about integration and not compartmentalisation

The role of the Church in an increasingly fragmented world must be to bring people together, for it is in the creativity of these connections that the energy for real change lies. Our experience of dealing with public finances – with five or six different government departments all at the same time – has demonstrated the wastage of limited public funds when human beings are dealt with in such a disconnected way. One of our artists calls it "painting by numbers", when the reality we are conscious of is of "real art". It is a reality in which people's educational, health, housing and employment needs are all inextricably bound up together, as one colour is mixed and merged with another.

Within the present building, spaces are claimed by specific groups – such as the nursery or artists – and are managed in a way that encourages a sense of ownership, but without privatisation. For example, the spaces are designed to be used by different groups simultaneously, so solutions have to be found which suit everyone. The need to share resources means that people have to rub shoulders with those they might otherwise prefer to ignore. The possibilities for integration begin to open up, and this allows the inevitable tension that arises from our diversity to become an opportunity for dialogue, rather than a block to communication.

There are very few spaces in our society where people from across the spectrum of life actually meet and connect: the general pattern is one of compartmentalisation. It is rare, for example, for the different disciplines – never mind ideologies – of art, health, education, the environment and enterprise to be so intrinsically linked. We have found, however, that it is only by creating a wide range of partnerships and pushing the process of integration deeper into our frameworks that regeneration initiatives, equal to the complexities of the issues, can be found.

5. The Third Millennium Church must be concerned about the designed environment

Do our church spaces surprise people or confirm their view of our hierarchy of values? Do our buildings speak of a theology truly in dialogue with the world through practical action or of a theology that stands over and above the real action, seeking only to impose its predetermined will?

The environment in which we live has a profound effect upon the way we feel about ourselves. The designed environment, therefore, is not only a physical statement of who we are but also of how we are valued by the planners. At Bromley by Bow we have designed the physical and emotional environment of the Centre to reflect the high value we place upon the people who use it. The building itself has become a statement of our commitment to creating environments based on integration, creativity and excellence.

6. A Third Millennium Church must be about quality and excellence

When designing project environments, quality and excellence are the two values we have emphasised. The buildings are designed and furnished to a high standard, using wood and quality materials, and we have surrounded the project with works of art to instil a sense of beauty and inspiration. This is in stark contrast to the cheap, degenerate environment of the surrounding area – and environment that serves simply to reinforce the sense of failure that has undermined this community for decades.

Our aim is to lift the low self-esteem of individuals by creating opportunities for excellence and achievement and to open up the world of possibilities by encouraging people to dream. It is our view that everyone has something to contribute to community life, and the simple act of expecting people to achieve rather than fail has enabled dreams to become reality. An important aspect of this approach is to recognise that many people in the inner city have been damaged by decades of inadequate resourcing, and that people's dreams reflect this low sense of expectation. The whole process of enabling dreams to soar is dependent on creating opportunities that are beyond either expectation or experience. Instead of asking people what they would like to do, our approach is to present opportunities which are different or unusual and which have the effect of opening up new experiences – for example, going to the Sinai Desert or to an art gallery or to the Ritz for afternoon tea. An important part of this process is to offer enough support to make the impossible become a reality, and it is here that the arts have a critical role to play.

7. A Third Millennium Church must take on the media on its own terms

The young people we work with live in a world full of opportunity and excitement that they see every day on their television screens. Yet they have no access. Crime can be quite exciting; it gives quite a buzz when there is little else to do. The Bromley by Bow Centre has no table tennis or snooker tables. We do, however, take young people across the Sinai Desert. We have also taken 15 young people on an ocean-going yacht across the English Channel. On both these occaisions, young people – many of whom have failed in traditional education – come back telling of an amazing experience. Lessons have been learnt about teamwork, interdependency, the natural world, human relationships and personal aspirations, etc. Eyes have been opened to the wider world and the rich possibilities it has in store for them that, until now, have only been accessible through the press of a button.

Such activities have borne much fruit as young people have moved on from these experiences and begun to play a constructive part in the life of their community. Young people in the East End do not need patronising by local youth workers taking them on day trips to a seaside resort. They do not need aspirin; they need to be offered the best wine, to know the choices and possibilities that exist in the world. They need to know that they are not simply passive observers but active participants.

8. The Third Millennium Church must recognise the opportunities for change that the partnership culture is creating

We were recently responsible for taking a group of middle managers from the NatWest and a group of *Big Issue* sellers across the Sinai Desert together. One night, around the campfire, conversation moved to people's backgrounds. It transpired that the father of one of the middle managers had been a dustbin man, while the father of one of the sellers had been a senior barrister. The developing relationships between the voluntary sector, the public sector and the business community have enabled many of us to begin to the grasp the complexity of the world we now live in. We have seen how our neat assumptions about each other no longer hold water. In the desert, where there is little to distract, we see each other clearly. We in Bromley by Bow embrace that complexity, for it is the road to the future.

The business community has certainly taught us a great deal about how organisations work and the connections between the creation of market capital and social capital. We believe that we have also taught some of our business partners something – about how inner city communities work and about the vested interests that can be harvested for everyone's good if only we work together.

9. The Third Millennium Church must join with its local communities in exploring new community values and ideas

New ideas and values don't come out of the clouds but through the interaction of the most unlikely partners. A partnership has been brought together in Bromley by Bow to design and build a new children's play area in the three-acre park. A group of local young people are working with a scientist from the department of haematology at Great Ormond Street Children's Hospital and artists from the Bromley by Bow Centre are collaborating with scientists and engineers from Aldermaston Nuclear Weapons Site to design the play area. The project is entitled The Rivers Within and has been sponsored by COPUS, the body concerned with the public understanding of science. This initiative is not about an academic talking shop; it is a practical opportunity for scientists, artists and children (the next generation) to explore each other's worlds and disciplines, each other's values and ideas, and to work together on a very practical task.

When the project is completed we will build a play space which, in an amusing way, practically illustrates the biological and human workings of the body. The play equipment might include a DNA ladder, teeth stepping stones, a bouncing tummy, a brain maze, and so on.

For many in our society the academic world has lost its way; science often feels disconnected, challenging our values and offering us choices which dazzle our moral senses. Yet it plays such a crucial role in all our lives. Theology, once the science of the church, exhibits many of the same disconnections. Both these important disciplines need opportunities for practical engagement, opportunities to move from speculation to incarnation.

10. The Third Millennium Church must continue to explore the place of liturgy and worship

During the last 14 years, the church in Bromley by Bow has explored in many different settings the role and function of liturgy. We have rejected what some call a "happy-clappy" style, in favour of a more reflective order built around the Eucharist. Many of the liturgies we have written over the years have been developed with local people and have attempted to express their aspirations and concerns. They have drawn upon the great liturgical traditions of the church which, when explained, have not been found to be irrelevant.

A regular liturgical pattern to our life, built around Sunday morning worship and evening prayer, has provided a continuity and rhythm to our lives. It has offered us a wider perspective to the demanding context in which we are placed and has enabled many of us to engage in some depth with people's lives, without expecting them to become members.

In the chaotic world of the inner city, the liturgy – like our café, called "Pie in the Sky" – provides a reliable place where the bread of life can be shared, a place where stories can be told, where human beings connect, where the rhythm and melody of a community can be played out for all to see and hear. In Bromley by Bow, we try not to take ourselves too seriously. We often say we're just having fun, dancing to the music and living dangerously!

It has to be asked: Where do we go from here – in the steps of St Paul? My immediate answer is that the Bromley by Bow Centre now has a life of its own and I have been released to work with a small group of social entrepreneurs to share these experiences and those of others who have come to a similar conclusion. Myself, Adele Blakebrough, a Baptist minister and until recently the director of the Kaleidoscope project, and Helen Taylor-Thompson, formerly director and now president of the Mildmay Mission Hospital in Hackney, have come together to develop a Community Action Network. This is a relationship-based mutual support and learning network, using new technology which will connect social entrepreneurs working across the UK. We are also building a community action centre in our new offices in Haymarket, central London. Our aim is to develop these premises as a physical centre for social entrepreneurs, bringing together in one place organisations that are at the cutting edge of social change in Britain. We are also developing ten other such centres across the UK and a residential centre in the Cotswolds to explore the linkages between urban and rural Britain.

This attempt to consolidate a more people-centred entrepreneurial approach to social development has encouraged me to reflect recently and to understand a little more clearly the role of St Paul – arguably the church's first social entrepreneur – in the development of the Christian Church. I can remember at university finding St Paul's theology difficult to grasp, but as a practitioner building an active community I have increasingly come to understand his methods.

Paul travelled across Asia Minor establishing Christian communities, appointing people (not committees), giving them a lead and then moving on. He demanded of James (our Lord's

Brother), Peter and other senior leaders of the young Christian church living in Jerusalem, that they drop their traditions of Judaism – circumcision, the eating of certain foods, etc – and that they travel lightly into the future, embracing and engaging with the Gentile culture, heresy to many.

He eventually established a Christian Community in Rome, at the heart of the Roman Empire, to which eventually Peter and other leading church figures moved. By following St Paul into the future and engaging with the big cultural/religious issues of the day, they learnt to take risks, to put people before tradition and structures and to let go of much of the baggage of the past, giving the church a new future. It was Paul who discovered many new resources in the Gentile world and persuaded the Gentile churches to give financial support to the Jewish church in Jerusalem in order that it might survive.

Those of us involved in building the community action network are not claiming to be St Pauls, but we wish to remind the church of the entrepreneurial tradition from which it came and which, in our view, in this new time, it must now reclaim. The community action centre wants to support people within the churches who behave in an entrepreneurial way. We are seeking to connect them with a wider network of movers and shakers beyond the boundaries of the Christian church. We want to encourage people who are committed to build a more "can do" culture and to work in partnership with others to spread this way of working. A truly ecumenical church is concerned with "the whole inhabited earth". It does not live in isolation but in community.

Maybe the time has come for us to read again the writings of St Paul, to understand his actions as well as his words, and, as we enter the Third Millennium, to leave Jerusalem and head for Rome – with all the risks that meant for him and also mean for us.

Rev. Andrew Mawson is Chairman of the Bromley by Bow Centre in London's East End and Co-Director of Community Action Network (CAN).

Chapter Three

A friend in deed? From care to community

by Simon Barrow

What on earth are churches for? William Temple, a former Archbishop of Canterbury and leading Christian social thinker, once famously commented that the Church was the only club run largely for the benefit of those who did not belong to it. By this he meant that its activity was intended to focus firmly on the needs of the wider community which it was there to serve. However, outside the membership of the different Christian churches in Britain, such a view remains rather untypical.

Generally, church congregations are thought of – especially by the media – as strangely self-preoccupied groups of people. Their central activity, worship, involves rituals, concepts and beliefs that are increasingly strange to a secularised culture. They have their own peculiar language, procedures and organisational structures. Above all, they are symbolised, in the popular imagination, by large buildings, Sunday services, weddings and funerals, and a curious person called the vicar, who apparently runs the show. But for the most part, certainly in urban areas, what the church does seems unconnected with the vast majority of people's everyday life.

Somewhere at the back of the public mind, however, there is still a notion that the Church is (or ought to be) "caring". At the very least, the vicar or minister might be someone to turn to in times of real trouble or crisis – though for many, this is a last resort. And of course there are those important rites of passage. Even so, the boundaries of the churches' caring are perceived as narrow. People sometimes mention social events (jumble sales and tea parties for older people), or maybe provision of space for community groups. There are also vague notions of "help for the homeless". But that's about it.

Actually, many churches are routinely involved in a far wider range of community partnerships, services and initiatives than that caricature allows. Sometimes this involves more specialised services which local parishes and church agencies sponsor – employment projects and housing associations, for example.

In attempting to picture, explain, explore and provide a critique of what is sometimes called "the churches' traditional caring role", my primary reference will be the Anglican Church, which I know best. But I also seek to reflect the concerns and involvement of other traditions.

In order to understand the parameters of churches' current caring activity, it is important to consider its history. The end of the Second World War constituted a watershed for the churches in their relationship to neighbourhood, community and society. This was an era of massive reconstruction and cultural change. Social insurance ushered in by the Beveridge report, universal public education, the arrival of a National Health Service and the growth of mass consumerism through a technology-driven expansion of industry and public utilities changed the face of the country for good.

For the churches, especially the Church of England, this meant the beginning of the end of their dominant function in the social order. It is easy to forget that much of the fabric of social provision in Britain has its direct origins in the work of the church in the late 19th and early 20th centuries – in particular, schools, social work, hospitals and welfare assistance. But where private patronage once reigned, public provision and policy now stepped in. Old dependencies and allegiances were broken as the moral and social fabric of society shifted perceptibly in the war years. The church as carer – in the sense of public benefactor – withered significantly.

In this new post-war settlement the Church not only faced declining influence but also falling allegiance. While average family income doubled between 1950 and 1980 (with a corresponding growth in leisure activities), the membership of all Christian churches fell from 9.6 million to less than 7 million. So although the churches maintained an active voice in national public policy and some clear stakes in public life (notably church schools), their contribution was reduced.

By contrast, the importance of pastoral activity and local voluntary work grew considerably. This was accompanied by an increase in lay involvement in social ministry. After the war, religion increasingly became part of the private rather than public realm. But in response to Thatcherism and the end of post-war corporate consensus, new centres of activity in civil society have opened up. Now, perhaps surprisingly, the churches – rooted in the very local situations where regeneration is being focused – are being challenged to harness their voluntary strengths to new social partnerships.

It is important to understand the particular methods and ideas that govern the caring activities in which churches are involved today – from lunch clubs, informal counselling and neighbourhood visiting schemes, right through to crèches, mums' and toddlers' groups, lobby groups, and more organised forms of provision. Two central issues arise here. First, what resources have the churches to offer? Second, how do they see their role in relation to the wider community?

In terms of resources, almost all churches have three major things to contribute:

* *A congregation*: not just people who occupy pews on a Sunday morning, but a visible collective presence in the community, reflecting a diversity of people not often replicated by other organisations in society. Here is a potential pool of volunteers, a social centre, and a group of people with their own individual links, involvements and networks in the neighbourhood – be it a geographical area with certain common features and services, or the various communities of interest, such as clubs, associations and pressure groups. The congregation, as a point of gathering and dispersal, may be even more important in areas with few other centres for public assembly.

* *Buildings*: as well as being a site for worship, the church building and hall is increasingly being used for community events, meetings and activities, usually at comparatively low cost. It can also be a haven of beauty and tranquillity for local people.

* *Staff*: in addition to clergy, this often includes other locally resident, skilled people – youth leaders, lay workers and administrators (paid or volunteer) – who are available to respond to crises, contribute to community activities, and support other initiatives in which the church may be involved.

In the case of Anglican, Catholic, Methodist and some other churches, resources also flow through church structures – epitomised by specialist advisers and departments. Moreover, the parish system (for Anglicans, particularly) provides a geographical and organisational framework whereby a local congregation – hopefully, working with other churches ecumenically – takes responsibility for its links with a defined group of people and their networks of support. This can help to generate a sense of community when little else in our fragmented urban environment, particularly, exists to assist "togetherness'. Overall, then, the churches are perhaps the largest single base for voluntary, caring activity in the country.

It is not possible to reduce this variety of church caring activity to just one set of models, but four principal areas of practice stand out: pastoral work, befriending, service (ministry) and prophetic activity. It will immediately become apparent, purely from the words used, that to understand these roles requires a familiarity with the language and culture which generate them.

This is something which is frequently ignored in media and public discussion, in which an aversion to anything that smacks of "religious jargon" or "theology" leads commentators to try to pigeon-hole the churches' caring involvement under categories provided by social work. This risks seriously misrepresenting what it seeks to portray. Like it or not, what is done by churches in the community is shaped by the Christian language used to describe and account for it.

The most traditional role associated with the church is the "pastoral" one, often closely allied with the work of clergy, but increasingly carried out by a range of lay people with professional or voluntary experience outside the church. Significantly, the term "pastoral" – in spite of its quaint rural associations, derived from biblical language – has increasingly been used to denote generalist one-to-one care in secular organisations, particularly colleges and universities.

In Anglican and Protestant circles, pastoral work often means individual care, but the Catholic tradition uses the term to signify the wider engagement of church and community. The confusion is compounded by the fact that the discipline of "pastoral theology", as taught in church training institutions, usually embraces the whole dimension of practical Christian involvement in the world.

Church pastoral concern, for the daily welfare of people and families, has recently been influenced by the growth of "talking therapies" – counselling and psychoanalytic methods. Within congregations, and on courses offered by churches, use is made of the loosely Jungian Myers-Briggs personality type indicator, for instance. But it should not be forgotten that the fundamental basis of pastoral assistance offered by churches is spiritual guidance. This need not mean dogmatic, evangelising or heavily moralistic approaches (although in more conservative church environments it may). Rather, it indicates a starting point for support where human beings and their discontents are recognised as being shaped by a life journey towards (or away from) "the good" and God.

Peter Selby, the Anglican bishop of Worcester, is among those who have criticised the ideology of "neutrality" and individualism that has crept into church pastoral work lately. He argues for a more dialectical, critical approach whereby the pastor (lay or clergy) may be required to take sides against the oppressive forces (social, cultural, religious, political) constraining the person(s) seeking support.

The challenge to the church here is to move from assisting individuals to thinking of those individuals as people-in-community, with particular attention being paid to "the pasture" – the social terrain which forms, and sometimes shapes, their lives.

It is also important, both for people inside and outside the church, that a dialogue is maintained between pastoral practice rooted in "the cure of souls" in the Christian tradition and counselling techniques which have their basis in other world views. This will help to avoid the confusion of some approaches to what gets called "Christian counselling" – where specific theological interests are disguised through the neutralising language of therapy. Particularly for the sake of vulnerable people, agendas need to be open and attempts to manipulate strenuously avoided.

Similarly, though the language of pastoral care helpfully highlights the questions of life-direction and spiritual need in a tradition with deep symbolic roots, it carries the associated danger of breeding over-reliance. People are not sheep, and should not be treated as such. Pastoral care can also too readily be "clericalised", privileging the church agenda over human need. This is the alter ego of "professionalisation" within secular caring agencies.

Such dangers have gained increasing recognition in many churches. Consolidated attempts have been made in a number of congregations to develop and train "pastoral care teams" with a balance of skills and aptitudes – from bereavement counselling, care for the elderly and support for lone parents, right through to spiritual advice.

The second caring role for churches is that of "befriending". An extension of the person-to-person pastoral encounter into the community, befriending involves a longer-term commitment to a neighbourhood. Organised visiting schemes, collectively taking Holy Communion to the sick or infirm, days out and social events for the elderly are all examples. There can also be church participation in day centre facilities for the vulnerable, youth clubs, children's play schemes or sheltered housing projects. Personal involvement in support groups for the bereaved or for people with special needs may be run in association with local voluntary groups.

There is no hard and fast boundary between this work and pastoral care, but the approach is more neighbourhood-centred and will stem from involvement in the networks arising through a local church congregation. Indeed, much of it may be carried out by people who happen to belong to the church rather than by "the church" as a named body.

Befriending starts with people as and where they are. It tends to be proactive rather than reactive, and it concerns everyday conditions, not just pastoral emergencies. Sometimes, as a development of the pastoral role, it may lead to lasting supportive companionships akin to the Celtic tradition of "soul friends". More often than not, it is about helping to create a wider sense of community and well-being.

From the Church's point of view, this can originate from, or create, a "pastoral contract" between the Church and some other sectors of society – a residential home, for instance. In some cases this might be spelled out in writing, and will involve a stable pattern of relating, possibly a volunteer scheme, and a commitment by the Church to offer assistance and prayer on a regular basis. Here we have the inter-personal beginnings of what Christians call the ministry of *diakonia* (service to others) – the desire to bring healing and wholeness to human beings and their communities.

The chief issues that arise for this kind of befriending work are about the boundaries of charity. Is this activity being done for ulterior motives, or out of genuine friendship? Are people (especially vulnerable groups) able to contribute to the relationship and its outworking, or are they made reliant and passive by being "done good to" on a more organised scale? In what sense is the "contract" shared? Is it the initiative of a few enthusiasts, or is it more widely supported in church and neighbourhood? Is the community seen as a good in itself, or mainly as a "field of mission" for the church?

These are the types of question which may lead on to thought about more organised service provision, the next role which the Church can take on as part of its caring agenda. Here we move into a realm where tensions may arise between the language of "service" in the church and the culture of "service providing" in the wider community.

One of the key functions both of ordained and lay Christians in all church traditions is to "minister", a term which also identifies clergy in many Protestant denominations. It means, of course, "to serve", and in New Testament usage implies that Christians are to model themselves on Christ "who took the form of a servant" (Philippians 2.7). The point of service is to identify with, become involved in, and live for the good of all people. The early Christian inspiration was therefore for the church to become a servant-community deeply implicated in, but also distinctive within, the world. This represented – in theory, at least – a reversal of traditional patterns of domination within religion and society.

Much contemporary Christian ministry is, at best, a rather club-like, watered-down version of this vision, where "ministers" – particularly clergy – become seen more as adjuncts to the masters than as servants. But the more radical servant-community model, moving beyond support for the congregation or befriending in the neighbourhood, has inspired some creative experiments in collective care over the past 30 years. Rooted in this model is a great deal of church-related community development – involving both the cultivation of specialist projects to serve different sectors of the community and the encouragement of skills and ways of working so that people can effectively organise themselves in, say, tenants groups, job clubs or cultural associations.

However, there are at least two poles of constraint. The first is the continued dominance of an individualised, pastoral and church-centred understanding of ordained ministry as the controlling principle in Christian service. [cf. Greenwood, 1996] The other, for those aiming at a more outward-looking approach, is the entanglement and complexity of moving into the arena of organised communal provision – that is, linking in with the structures of statutory regulation, local authorities and voluntary services management.

It is not that these things lack merit – far from it. Indeed, the skills of social work, the values of equal opportunities and the demands of urban regeneration have often done much to challenge churches to widen their horizons and renew their self-understanding. But the levels of resource deployment and specialisation required can also detract from the enthusiasm, flexibility and critical spirit of popular neighbourhood initiatives. For example, the shift from voluntary involvement in setting up a community association to participation in a social housing scheme is a huge one. People buried in paperwork, committees, planning agreements and employment legislation have therefore been known to talk of "oppression by projects". Whether projects are the most appropriate use of the churches' energy is the key concern, not the undoubted importance of such ventures in themselves.

Often two rather different questions emerge at this juncture. One is whether (and in what way) the Church, instead of effectively becoming an arm of social service, might begin to create or demonstrate alternative forms of community life. And the other, different but not necessarily discontinuous, is about the need to challenge the treatment of vulnerable and excluded groups by society, rather then simply to patch up their wounds, either pastorally or through the provision of support services.

The former impulse, towards distinctive approaches to collective living arising from the church, should not be confused with an inward-facing "pious" culture. Rather, it may consist of developing practices – such as conflict resolution, resource sharing or care networks – which demonstrate new ways forward to other sectors and groups in society. When this happens, *diakonia* (service to others) is complemented by *koinonia*, the cultivation of a transforming community.

The Christian understanding, of course, is that *koinonia* arises from, and expresses, faith and hope in God, and therefore the future. It is a commitment to exhibit certain change-making and liberating characteristics which can offer extra possibilities to the world as a whole. *Koinonia*, Christians believe, is a sign – however modest – of the coming kingdom (or commonwealth) of God. It is the distinct, though not exclusive, face of the "servant community" which sees itself as responsible *for* society, but not always responsible *to* it. There is a reservation of the right to be different in the name of a wider good, which people of faith experience as coming from God.

A positive and attractive example of the building of *koinonia* in the wider community would be the brave actions of some churches and Christian groups in Northern Ireland, which – unlike many other churches, it must be said – have actively refused to be defined by sectarian and divisive loyalties and aspirations, either religious or political. There are also a number of small, ecumenically-supported attempts at "new ways of being church" occurring in different parts of Britain and Ireland, including experiments in interfaith collaboration and community-building. The "Building Bridges of Hope" project, under the auspices of Churches Together in Britain and Ireland, is currently gathering data and material from a cross-section of such experiments.

But what happens when frameworks of interpersonal care prove inadequate because of deep-seated human prejudice, violence or social injustice? Here, some churches and allied groups have taken what many of them describe as a "prophetic" stance.

In popular parlance, prophecy is usually understood to be foretelling the future. It more accurately means forth-telling, or truth-telling of a kind which calls into question the viability of the future as it is seen by the current status quo.

Over the past 20 years there has been a resurgence of commitment to the idea – evidenced strongly in the biblical tradition – that God has a special concern for those who are pushed to the margins of society. This is the basis of the "bias to the poor" – to use the term popularised by David Sheppard, high-profile former Anglican bishop of Liverpool – which acts as a systemic corrective and challenge to a divided and unequal society.

This language and commitment, arising specifically from the

Christian tradition, is much more radical in its implications than the present preoccupation with "social exclusion". It proceeds from a vision of interdependence and equality (*koinonia* writ large), rather than one of partial re-incorporation into a social order that may still remain hugely imbalanced in terms of power and wealth.

The prophetic model of church action, therefore, eschews purely ameliorative, individual and consensual care – opting instead (or in addition) for a stance of solidarity with, or advocacy for, groups of people "pushed out" by the prevailing order. This will include homeless people, the unemployed, low-income families, lone parents, migrants, refugees and discriminated-against ethnic communities. Pressure to change public policy through community organising, lobbying and direct action are the means used. Since the 1980s a number of churches have offered sanctuary to asylum seekers or refugees who are victims of unjust government immigration policy, for example. Many are also linked to broad issue-based alliances, such as Church Action on Poverty.

The prophetic principle is that "caring" is not the beneficence of a group of privileged people towards others who are less fortunate. It is, rather, care for the whole fabric of human relationships. Similarly, the purposes of God are not restricted to individuals, but extend to the flourishing of a corporate life that guarantees, and affords meaning to, human persons. This is why the final biblical vision is the coming of a "New Jerusalem" – a metropolis of healing, justice and peace in which, alone, God is rightly discovered.

What is really at stake in each of these four faces of the church-in-community? It is the very meaning of "caring" itself – namely, who cares for whom, by what mandate, how and to what ends? In most cases, with churches that exist in the pastoral and befriending modes, the direction of activity is from strength to weakness. There is an implicit split between carer and cared-for, provider and provided-for. The underlying assumption, however well-meaning, is that "we" (a group of able people with resources) care for "them" (a group of needy people lacking resources). Such a construct, buried deep in the language and practice of charity, is challenged by churches involved in "servant community" or "prophetic" activities, where the aim is to build human solidarity and break down social division. Service provision straddles these positions: it deals in need, but also seeks to create mutuality.

And what of the self-interest of the Church as a body with a particular message to proclaim? We have already seen how much Christian language conditions practice. But what is the ultimate agenda? Disinterested service or proselytism? The expansion of the church, the rescue of souls, or transformation for the world? How these questions are addressed depends on the awareness of the particular churches involved, both socially (how they see power operating in society) and religiously (how they interpret the faith that shapes their caring activity).

While it is difficult to generalise, it is not unreasonable to suggest, for example, that churches preoccupied wholly with one-way, individual donor activity based on helping "people in need" – still a majority, in spite of the considerable expansion of other models – tend to see such need as mainly a matter of moral inadequacy or misfortune. They are also likely to understand their activity through a version of the Christian message focusing on personal faith mediated by an exclusive church. By contrast, Christians involved in campaigning and advocacy are more likely to see people's needs as generated through social inequality or injustice, and will usually understand their responsive activity as part of a Christian hope for the renewal of the whole human community, not just the extrication of a few "souls" from it or the enlarging of the church within it.

Here we are dealing with incommensurate outlooks – one primarily individualistic and privileged, the other primarily social and anti-exclusive. In many cases, attitudes and motives will be more mixed or inchoate than this polarity suggests. Nonetheless, these basic fault lines persist within church-based caring activity, and a test of its maturity is its ability to confront such issues openly and honestly. For, in addition to *diakonia* (offering service) and *koinonia* (creating community), the traditional four-fold ministry of the church also involves *kerygma* (the announcing of the Gospel, or "Good News" of God's love) and *leituorgia* (the liturgy, or "work of the people").

This automatically begs the question – one which rages throughout the Bible and in the history of Christian mission – about who this Good News is for, and whether the liturgy is depicting God's concern for all, or just for a "chosen" few? To those outside the faith, this may look suspiciously like a "churchy" debate, but it profoundly effects the style and scope of community activity supported by the church. It also relates to inescapable questions about the nature, purpose and boundaries of human community which those operating from a secular perspective will also be required to face in issues, for example, about hardened criminals, sex offenders, violent people and those suffering mental disturbance.

This brings us to the three final questions which must be posed about any caring activity carried out from, or supported by, institutional churches. Does it breed dependence? Is it sustainable? Is it adequate? Here we are probing much deeper than an appraisal of specific strengths and weaknesses. We are inquiring about the credibility of the whole enterprise.

The first question asks whether church-based caring can ultimately be anything other than the perpetuation of privilege for the churches and the denial of rights for those they serve. Perhaps this sounds rather harsh, but it is how many secular agencies and activists still feel about church involvement in community action. In order for it not to be the case there must be a substantive sharing of the "ownership" of caring activities by others in the locality. There must be a breaking down of the walls – mental and physical – which separate the church from community, and a definite move beyond the debasing aspects of charity, whereby those on the receiving end of service, ministry or befriending are required to sacrifice their dignity, particularity and autonomy as part of the process of giving and receiving.

There are real signs in some areas – inner city ones especially – that this is happening. Projects like Praxis in Bethnal Green, East London, which focus on the concerns of migrants, refugees and others dislocated by the mobility of the global city, show that it is possible for church-centred agendas to give way to community-centred ones. But such initiatives are few, and they raise huge issues for the re-definition of Christian mission and identity in a plural world.

The second question concerns the fate of institutional churches per se, and their consequent viability as a base for community engagement. Both mainline denominational and ecumenical structures in Britain have been struggling for some time. Many of our churches are, frankly, dying. They have been moving out of the cities to the suburbs, losing resources, and finding themselves bound by the maintenance and re-engineering of cumbersome buildings. Meanwhile, more localised, fragmentary and informal types of religiosity – from the Christian charismatic movement to so-called "new age" spiritualities – have been expanding their influence and membership.

It is now clear that more adaptive forms of church life are needed – ones which seek to reinvest in the strengths of what now is (concern for a geographical area, strong regional networks, a commitment to mutual support, the quest for shared vision) while cultivating a preparedness to experiment much more boldly (joint ownership of property, new kinds of intentional religious community, social alliances, the creation of local community resource centres).

In the case of the Church of England, this will most likely involve abandoning the status and mentality of "establishment" which makes ecumenism, community collaboration and structural change so difficult. More generally, it may involve churches resisting the temptation to fill the vacuum in restructured public services with activity aimed at strengthening civil society as a whole.

The third question is about whether too much church-based caring activity substitutes piecemeal "doing good" for the development of a new, coherent understanding of "the good". The real importance of church community involvement may lie much more in its ability to construct, and contribute to, a radical and distinctive picture of an *alternative* community (locally, regionally, trans-regionally, globally) than in the endless pursuit of better projects and works. This may be especially the case in the face of blandishments both from the post-1997 Labour government and from the Conservative Party leader, William Hague (in November 1998), to restore the "historic role" of the churches as a "voluntary social agency", which many will see as, in part, a cipher for displacing statutory provision.

If the Christian message is founded in a "divine reversal" – whereby outsiders become insiders, the weak are strengthened and the last are put first – then there must be considerable scope for developing that kind of vision in dialogue with other groups, religious and otherwise. This will lend priority to locally-rooted initiatives that share and promote levelling values – everything from resource-exchange schemes to shared advocacy groups.

The illusions of endless consumer expansion and the conceits of limitless individual autonomy also need to be challenged by languages and practices of human "covenant" (rather than juridical or financial "contract") and "communion" (rather than chaos or competition). Religious language and perspectives, obscure though they may first seem, have a vital role in all this.

If the lines of constructive critique I have outlined are correct, then the future for church-related caring activity will be found in a shift from primarily ethnic to civic community involvement. That is, away from working mainly alongside people from "our group" (Christians) and towards active collaboration with those of different faith, lifestyle or background. The aim will be to re-found appropriate forms of human-scale community in the midst of economic change, social division and cultural pluralism. This in turn will require forsaking many existing hierarchical church agendas for the sake of wider, experimental social alliances.

Given the Christian requirement to examine what kind of spirit and beliefs are needed to adequately ground and sustain human community, it will also be necessary to cultivate new forms of religious life: fresh Gospel-style communities [cf. Arbuckle, 1991]. Some have begun to use the term "macro-ecumenism" to describe this overarching concern for the *oikos* – meaning "human household", from which the word "ecumenism" comes. This is the larger goal for which church caring – if it really is to benefit the whole community – should strive.

Simon Barrow is associate secretary of the Churches' Commission on Mission at Churches Together in Britain and Ireland. He teaches at the South-East Institute for Theological Education and was formerly the adult education and training officer for Southwark Anglican Diocese.

Selected reading
Gerald A Arbuckle *Grieving for Change* (Mowbray, 1991)
Robin Greenwood *Practising Community: the Task of the Local Church* (SPCK, 1996)
Malcolm Grundy *Community Work: A Handbook* (Mowbray, 1995)
Paulos Mar Gregorios *The Meaning and Nature of Diakonia* (World Council of Churches, 1988)

Peter Mathew *The Local Church in the New Reformation* (Australian Frontier, 1966)

Loren B Mead *The Once and Future Church* (Alban Institute, USA, 1994)

Praxis Annual Reports, 1998-9 and 1999-2000

Malcolm Smart *Opportunity in Community* (British Council of Churches, 1995)

Peter Selby *Liberating God: Private Care and Public Struggle* (SPCK, 1983)

Chapter Four

Casting the Net: Virtual and real

by Jim McDonnell

Every new communication technology raises Utopian hopes, and at the same time arouses scepticism and apprehension. Gutenberg's invention of printing from moveable type in the 15th century was welcomed as a marvellous device for spreading learning and religious truth. But Gutenberg's home city of Mainz, in Germany, was also the first to set up an official office of censorship when it was realised how easily the printing press could spread heretical as well as orthodox views. Nearly 400 years later, in 1848, Samuel Morse spoke of the power of the electric telegraph to bring the people of America together into one "neighbourhood". Other commentators of the time hailed it as a herald of a new era of universal communication and community. The sceptics, on the other hand, saw it bringing little improvement in the quality or relevance of the messages being communicated. As the American writer and social critic Thoreau was to remark caustically a few years later about the proposal to build the first transatlantic submarine cable, "We are eager to tunnel under the Atlantic and bring the Old World some weeks nearer to the New; but perchance the first news that will leak through into the broad, flapping American ear will be that the Princess Adelaide has the whooping cough."

Today, reactions to and comments on the growth and expansion of the Internet and its increasing use as a publishing medium by groups and individuals has begun to stimulate a similar mixture of reactions. Those who are excited by the Internet see it as a system which will, this time, increase everyone's access to information and knowledge, improve global understanding, strengthen community bonds, encourage social tolerance and open up new economic possibilities. The more sceptical fear a growing inequality between "information rich" and "information poor", the diminution of personal privacy, increasing commercialisation of the Internet and weakening of communities as people become more attached to computers than people.

Before we rush to decide on which side of these debates we stand it is worth remembering that, as the American historian Elizabeth Eisenstein has shown in her study of the cultural consequences of Gutenberg's invention, the disturbance caused by a new technological design to its cultural ambience is never in one direction only. Thus, although print ensured that the new learning of the Renaissance was disseminated rapidly through European culture, it also ensured that the old learning of the Middle Ages was preserved and made more widely available. In both cases, printing's duplicating power meant that, for the first time, the texts of old and new learning could be easily preserved, compared, edited, annotated, criticised and corrected, while their insights could be built upon by new thinkers and scholars.

As with learning, so too the impact of printing on matters of belief was double-edged. Printed tracts, pamphlets, treatises and vernacular editions of the Bible became a major factor in the rapid spread of the Reformation, but equally, missals, breviaries, catechisms and apologetic works helped to promote the Catholic Counter Reformation. Print helped to promote a belief in the reliability and objectivity of science by standardising scientific knowledge and so making the natural world seem ultimately predictable and orderly. By contrast, the printing of variant texts of Scripture and the wider dissemination of conflicting religious views encouraged a more sceptical view of established Christian beliefs.

There is no doubt that printing has had a profound effect on modern culture. How profound an impact the Internet will have is still to be seen. The observations of Eisenstein about the doubled-edged nature of printing's impact on our culture offers us a model for thinking about how groups are using the Internet and how they might be influenced by it. It is unlikely that the Internet will be as benign in its effects as its supporters hope, or as pernicious as its critics fear. The precise consequences of the Internet will vary as the cultural ambience within which it operates varies. The effects of the Internet on all communities, including churches, will be multi-dimensional and often contradictory.

We may deplore the illiberal resort to censorship of church and state in the 15th century and consider that Thoreau was too dismissive of the potential of the telegraph, but the censors and Thoreau both alert us to the key issue. Do improvements in the technical systems of communication actually enhance the quality of the content of communication? However impressive the Internet is as a technology, its potential to produce the community benefits we seek will depend upon how it is used, regulated and integrated with other modes of communication. Different community structures will interact with the Internet in different ways and the potential of the Internet will stimulate communities to respond in accordance with their perceived needs and ambitions. Of course, like any other new technological design, the Internet will produce unintended and, as of today, unknown consequences.

However, before we decide what the impact of the Internet will be we need first to explore just what the Internet actually is. Then we can consider what the churches are currently doing to establish a presence on the Internet. This information will provide us with the context in which to explore some of the questions about the extent to which the Internet is encouraging the emergence of a new form of community – and, indeed, whether the idea of "community" can properly be applied to social interactions mediated through the Internet. Finally, we shall consider what might be the key issues that the churches should be addressing if they want to ensure that the Internet supports and enhances communities and community life.

As its name suggests, the Internet is an international network of computer networks, linked by the global telephone system. It is the world's fastest growing communications medium. In January 1990, there were a little under 3.5 million people using some form of computer mediated communication and about a third of them had full access to the Internet. In April 1998, it was estimated that there were 115.75 million users of the Internet worldwide. Of these, 70 million were in North America and 23 million in Europe. The predications are that, by the year 2000, there will be more than 800 million Internet users.

According to a National Opinion Poll survey in 1997, nearly a million households in Britain had access to the Internet in June 1997. Around one in 25 of all households in Britain are now linked to the Internet, and around nine million British adults are expected to have used the Internet by June 1998. In addition, the use of the Internet in schools and colleges is growing, not least because it is being heavily promoted by the government.

There are a number of reasons for the Internet's popular success. It provides a whole range of services: news, travel information, documents, free software, pictures, sounds, magazines and electronic mail. Through the Internet, and from the comfort of your home (or office!), you can play interactive games with other players from around the world. You can buy books, CDs, videos, book airline tickets, arrange holidays, build friendships or even fall in love.

The most popular use of the net is for electronic mail (email), written messages composed on the computer and sent in electronic form over the telephone network to other Internet users. Millions of such messages are sent through the net each day. The great advantages of email are that the same messages can be sent to many people at the same time and that, unlike post, the cost of sending the message is independent of the distance travelled. Moreover, each email user has his or her own electronic mail box. Messages are kept in this mail box on a central computer until the addressee dials in and collects the waiting correspondence. The addressee can scan his or her mail and decide whether to print it out, forward it to another mail box or fax machine, file it on the computer or delete it entirely. Through email, people are easily and quickly able to get in touch with colleagues, friends, acquaintances and even complete strangers across the world.

Electronic mail, however, does not have quite the glamorous connotations of the World Wide Web (www). The Web is simply that part of the Internet which allows computer users to engage in electronic publishing. It is a global system for publishing electronic pages which can contain text, graphics, sounds and video images. Web pages are given computer addresses so that the user can easily move from Web page to Web page simply by using a mouse to click on words highlighted on screen. These words are links to a sophisticated cross-referencing system known as hypertext. The practice known as "surfing" the Web refers to this process of using hypertext links to move between pages on different Web sites.

The Web has rapidly become almost synonymous with the Internet. In June 1993, there were only 130 Web sites (collections of Web pages) on the Internet; now there are millions. At the start, only researchers, scientists and academic users could produce Web pages; today, anyone with a PC, a telephone, modem and a word processing package can publish their own pages. The Web is becoming increasingly popular among all kinds of users. The 1997 NOP survey found that just over three million British Internet users had used the Web during the previous four weeks – a figure which represented a threefold growth over an 18-month period. Of these three million people, some 34 per cent were home users.

But what of Christian churches on the Internet? Like printing, the Internet has enabled a huge variety of people and institutions to become producers of texts. Unlike printing, however, the production of these texts is relatively simple. Even though there are multitudes of intermediaries offering to design, construct and market Web pages, huge numbers of groups and individuals are producing their own Web pages with simple word processing tools.

Religious groups of all forms and beliefs have embraced with enthusiasm these publishing possibilities of the Web. All the major faiths have Web pages of varying degrees of sophistication and comprehensiveness. The interested explorer can find information on Islam and the Muslim community through the Islamic Gateway (www.unmah.org.uk) and on Buddhism through the Buddhist Info Web (www.dharmanet.org). The Jewish community has also embraced the Web with enthusiasm and a good example of a lively and informative Web site is Maven (www.maven.co.il). Web sites on Hinduism are less frequent and harder to find, but a good example is the one maintained by Hinduism Today (www.hinduismtoday.kauai.hi.us). A pioneering Web site is maintained by the Multi-Faith Network (www.multifaith.net), bringing together information and links to a wide variety of religious traditions in the UK. In addition, huge numbers of smaller cults and religious groups have found the Internet a fertile soil in which to plant their beliefs in everything from UFOs to the dawn of the New Age.

Not surprisingly, like printing, the Web has appealed strongly to Christian groups. The Internet offers Christian communities of all kinds and sizes the opportunity to put themselves and their views before a wider world. It has been estimated that more than 80 per cent of mainstream religious Web sites are Christian. In the words of the author Jeff Zaleski, "If cyberspace is a digital ocean, then Christianity online is its tidal wave". A recent search through the Web yielded more than 1.8 million document references to the name Jesus, over 4 million to "Christian" and nearly 4 million to "Church". By comparison, the search term "sex" yielded more than 7 million references, but, more encouragingly, the term "community" returned nearly 16 million documents.

Churches, church-related organisations and individual church members across the world are all involved with the Internet. Many church organisations and church members use the Internet for email, and increasingly they are also setting up their own Web pages to offer information, inspiration and various forms of enlightenment. Most famously, perhaps, the Vatican has set up its own Web site, where you can read press releases, the Pope's speeches and encyclicals, and take a virtual tour of the Vatican museums. In Britain, all the major churches, as well as a host of fellowships and smaller denominations, have their own Web pages, as do organisations such as the Church Urban Fund, the Children's Society, the Bible Society, Cafod and Christian Aid. Dioceses, parishes and individual churches publish their news and information on the Web. So too do special interest groups, religious orders, retreat houses and any church-linked organisation that believes it has a message to convey. Individual clergy and lay people have pages also.

Even a cursory exploration of the Web soon reveals the extent to which it is now a global phenomenon. Groups and individuals in many different countries have chosen to advertise themselves and their communities on the Web. For example, a brief search through the Cross Search Web site (www.crosssearch.com), one of the many sites dedicated to acting as directories to other resources, indicated the addresses of Web pages created by churches in 21 countries, from Australia to the USA. The first few sites listed give a taste of the range covered, such as: Across Pacific & Asia (listing of churches, cell groups, ministries, service opportunities, etc); African web sites; Anglican Diocese of Guinea; Calvary Chapel, Ukraine; Calvary International Baptist Church, Taipei (with Real Audio preaching on the site); Celtic Christianity; Chilliwack Full Gospel Assembly, etc. This pattern is repeated time and again. The UK pages from Cross Search, for example, list Anglican and Catholic parishes, the Salvation Army, Baptist, Presbyterian, Pentecostal, Community, Seventh-Day

Adventist churches, Christian Unions at different universities, various Fellowships, and other ministries.

However, access to such a range and variety of information does not in itself mean that old community structures and patterns are being changed. These pages are put on the Web by communities which generally have little interest in breaking out of old denominational boundaries. The Internet is attractive to such groups because it offers a chance to promote existing messages to a new audience, and to do so using a new technology. In the same way that religious groups first used print, and later radio and television, the Web pages of most churches and other groups are designed as publicity to replicate existing ideas and reinforce existing communities – and, if possible, to attract new members and supporters. However technically sophisticated and visually elaborate these Web pages are, they are not radical departures in terms of community.

Through the Internet, Christian communities, like so many other organisations, are forming varieties of communication networks. The idea of building an Internet network of communities is particularly attractive to some of the New Churches, which are already based around a network model of community organisation. In Britain, for example, Pioneer has invested a good deal of effort in building up an extensive, and global, Internet presence. On its Web Home Page (www.pioneer.org.uk), Pioneer defines itself as "a network of churches and a team of men and women committed to dynamic and effective Christianity".

Pioneer seeks to represent the Christian faith in non-religious and culturally relevant ways. Its team is led by Gerald Coates and "at its heart is a network of partnership churches who are seeking to be effective, growing communities involved in prayer evangelism, church planting and social action. Partnership is an expression of mutual and growing relationship between national/regional apostolic teams and local church leadership teams". Pioneer has partnership churches across the UK and in France, Switzerland and Canada, and has associate churches in Germany and the USA. Pioneer is also involved in supporting a number of churches and projects in many other nations.

This network model is promoted by a growing number of churches and communities which often call themselves fellowships or networks. Most of these networks are also designed to strengthen existing links between already established communities. Others, however, are being formed by people who wish to challenge existing models of control and authority and to build up new kinds of community. The Internet provides them with an opportunity to build links with like-minded people. It is particularly useful for those dissenting groups which may have relatively small numbers of members scattered across a variety of geographical locations. In Britain, for example, the Catholic group We Are Church (www.we-are-church.org) has set up a Web site to provide information and to link with similar groups in Germany, Austria, Spain and Canada. In this respect, this group is similar to any other special interest group that offers to put like-minded people in touch with one another and to disseminate information that might be of common interest.

Some groups, however, have taken the use of the Web one step further. They have set up what are being called virtual communities: that is, the community only exists on and through the Internet itself. These "virtual" communities exist primarily as "text based" interactions. In this sense, a group has actually created a "world" out of information that can be accessed by anyone on the Internet. The famous example of such a virtual community is French Bishop Jacques Gaillot's virtual diocese of Partenia.

Partenia's Home Page (www.partenia.org) calls itself a Diocese Without Frontiers. It is, in this respect, a perfect example of the power of the Internet to transcend national and cultural boundaries. Unlike other Internet communities, however, there is no Diocese of Partenia outside the Net. Indeed, when Bishop Gaillot was dismissed by the Pope from the Diocese of Evreux for his liberal views, he was given the titular see of Partenia precisely because it had ceased to exist. (It was originally a small Christian community in the Sahara and disappeared around the 5th century). But Partenia now is Gaillot and his views. The Web site gets about 5,000 hits (people accessing the page) a month. In his first year on-line, Gaillot received more than 3,000 emails, and over 300 other sites have set up links to Partenia.

The existence of Partenia opens up a huge set of questions about what constitutes a Christian community on the Internet. Discussion is immediately hampered, however, by the fact that the word community is such a slippery term. We talk about the local community – the place where we live; we talk about communities of interest – from football to fly fishing; we refer to the gay community, the Jewish community, the political community, the Christian community, and so on. Everywhere we turn there is some community or other. So many uses of the term community, so many realities covered by such a simple word. But when we start to take a closer look at what it means to speak of Church communities on the Internet, it is time to examine the concept in more depth.

The question of community is particularly pertinent for the Christian churches. The advent of radio and television and the so-called "electronic church" has prompted a good deal of heart searching about the nature of authentic Christian community. Much agonising has gone on about the extent to which radio listeners or television viewers can be said to be members of a community if they are not physically present among other members of the community. Moreover, most Christian communities have generally set quite strict rules to determine who is and who isn't a member of the community. The Internet, like television, challenges both the notion of physical presence as essential and makes it difficult to determine who is or is not a member.

As theologian Debbie Gaunt remarks, "in cyberspace, the notion of community is still being defined. In *The Virtual Community* (1993), Rheingold considers that 'the WELL [an early Internet academic network] was an authentic community because it was grounded in [his] everyday physical world'. Others would argue that a particular section of the Internet – say, a usenet news group – constitutes an authentic online community precisely because it does not depend on physical contact, but on a sharing of ideas. My view is that if we cannot yet agree what sort of community exists on the Internet, we are not in any position to define its parameters."

Is the word community, in the Internet context, any more than a fancy way of saying that churches use the Internet as a communications link between people in different churches from different locations? Is there any real difference between an Internet "community" and an Internet "network"? Can there be a real community on the Internet? How significant for people in church communities is the Christian Church's entry into the Internet world?

In order to pursue the question of the relationship between

the Internet and the Christian community we need some working definition of community. Arguing that the term community is simply inappropriate in the context of the Internet seems the least satisfactory approach. It seems not to take into account that many people feel themselves to be a part of online communities. It also fails to acknowledge the extent to which groups on the Internet refer to themselves as communities.

The definition of community offered by the Jesuit theologian and philosopher Bernard Lonergan seems helpful: "By a community is not meant a number of people within a frontier. Community means people with a common field of experience, with a common or at least complementary way of understanding people and things, with common judgments and aims." To be a member of community, in this sense, is first of all to recognise and wish to be part of "a community that is the carrier of a common world mediated by meaning and motivated by values".

In the Lonergan sense, therefore, the "virtual diocese" of Bishop Gaillot can claim to be one manifestation of community and the network of Pioneer churches can claim to be another expression of the concept. The two communities are similar, in that both are attempting to build a "common world" for those who wish to belong to them. They differ in the degree to which members of the community interact directly with one another, either face-to-face as members of real world communities or as participants in online discussions or as correspondents via email. The greater the extent of interaction, the greater the degree of community cohesion – and the more, one could argue, that the community is likely to encourage personal attachment and commitment.

One advantage of the Internet for relatively small groups such as We Are Church, Pioneer or Gaillot's virtual diocese is that, on the Internet, all groups have equal weight and standing. A New Church has as substantial a presence on the Internet as the Church of England; a network of liberal Catholics has a chance to produce a Web site that will be as accessible as, and perhaps more attractive than, the Vatican's. (This equality of standing and authority with what often they see as "subversive" or "undesirable" groups, is, of course, what makes established communities and churches apprehensive about the Web.) The advantages, in terms of public recognition and resources, are still with the larger groups, but the nature of the Internet means that there are more opportunities for different voices to be heard.

But, for voices to be heard, they must be sought out. The structure of the Internet is crucially determined by the extent to which particular Web sites are linked by hypertext to other sites. Even when groups make extensive efforts to ensure that their pages are accessible from as many sources as possible, however, there is no guarantee that they will attract (or keep) new friends. From the user's perspective, listings of Web addresses of different kinds of groups and organisations are simply the same kind of juxtaposition that one might get in a telephone directory. Seeing the names of such diverse groups placed together does not automatically mean that people will rush to explore unfamiliar territory. Indeed, the very number of choices available to the Internet user may encourage him or her to "surf" only in well-charted waters, looking only for "Catholic" or "Pentecostal" pages, for example, and ignoring links that might take them into unknown places where cherished beliefs might be challenged. It is hard to know how many people are stimulated by the ease of searching for information on the Internet to consciously to seek out new ideas and form new networks of information and personal relationships. In this way, the very success of the Internet in attracting so many people to produce information may actually be intimidating and inhibiting to the new user.

The wealth of information available on the Internet has certainly been raised as a matter of concern by a number of commentators. No doubt there were voices raised in the 15th century about the super abundance of information available and the impossibility of coping. This century has seen an increasing awareness that we may be drowning in too much information. In the words of the author Günther Grass, "Information networks straddle the world. Nothing remains concealed. But the sheer volume of information dissolves the information. We are unable to take it all in."

A similarly pessimistic view was expressed by the former Archbishop of York, Dr John Habgood. In 1995, he put forward the case that the Internet would be the cause of serious problems "The sheer quantity of available information, quite apart from the way it is presented, can have a disorienting effect," he said. "To be overloaded with information reinforces the sense that knowledge is just an endless succession of human opinions, and that there are no abiding truths and principles by which human beings ought to live."

Habgood expresses the age-old fear of the defenders of authority that a new technology is undermining established truths and orthodoxies. He is afraid that the use of the Internet is reinforcing relativism and subjectivism, and so undermining the claims of religious communities to be the authoritative guardians and interpreters of religious and moral truths. How far he is right to be afraid is a moot point. Certainly the points he raises have to be taken seriously, particularly when one considers how the advent of hypertext has intensified the sense that every text is impermanent and elusive.

To some extent, the emergence of hypertext can be seen as a partial reversal of the process begun by printing. For printing made it possible to conceive of the Bible as a fixed, authoritative, definitive text which could be endlessly duplicated. And even if there were varying translations and variant readings, it was still possible to conceive the notion of an ideal edition that would reconcile all possible readings. Hypertext, however, encourages the reader to create their own text out of a variety of sources. It is a process of which the Belgian philosopher, Raoul Vaneigem, would have approved when he wrote: "Ideally, a book would have no order to it, and the reader would have to discover his own."

Habgood sees such freedom to create new worlds as a danger: "In their own way, the media contribute to the disorientation I have been describing, simply by virtue of the quantity of images and ideas which can wash over those exposed to them.... It is the same point I was making recently about the Internet. To have almost limitless power to call up any image, to convey and receive information without any restraints, to create, as it were, one's own world, could reinforce the dangerous perception that life has no purpose beyond individual self-gratification."

The creation of "one's own world" on the Internet has, of course, similarities with the imaginative process of creating one's own world in print. Individuals and groups have created their own imaginative and intellectual realities for centuries. When these realities have clashed with the dominant culture, the result has been civil and cultural conflict. Galileo, Darwin, Marx and Freud were all criticised in very similar terms to the ones used by Habgood. So, in one sense, the problem can be seen as an old dilemma appearing in a new guise.

To this extent, one can discount the apocalyptic warnings that the Internet is going to radically undermine existing ecclesial and other authority structures and give birth to decentralised democratic communities. The Internet joins the telegraph, the telephone, the radio and the television as a technology of communication inspiring both fear and fervid Utopian hope. Established church communities and authorities will undoubtedly have to adapt their ways of operating and thinking to take into account these new realities. The churches will have to adapt to the challenge of the Internet, in the same way that they have adapted to other communication technologies. There are signs that this necessity is already being recognised and acted upon.

In the first place, the churches need to avoid encouraging a polarisation between "real" and "virtual" communities. The task of the churches is to build up community links and community feeling. They are already using the Internet to support existing "real world" communities by providing information and products for their members. Email is already an important tool of communication, and many church members find belonging to Internet chat "forums" and "news groups" stimulating and enriching. These activities can happily co-exist with the provision of services on the Internet which demand a much lower level of participation but offer the Web surfer more than a data base to access.

Partenia's success as a "virtual community" may be because it invites people to feel part of a community of thought and feeling but leaves them free to decide whether and when to reveal themselves and their opinions. (The Samaritans have discovered recently that many people find it easier to contact them via email than by telephone. The computer offers a blessed anonymity to those in distress.) And when people wish to make contact with the heart of this "virtual community" they have only to click their mouse and send an email. There is also an undoubted attraction exercised by the personality of Jacques Gaillot, a personality which is mediated through his Web pages. The Web in this sense, therefore, offers the possibility both of personal encounter and impersonal freedom. One can "belong" and remain independent at the same time. But is this so different from what happens in "real world" communities? All communities are composed of people with varying degrees of involvement. The Internet does not alter that basic reality, but it does open up the potential catchment area for the community to the whole world. For this reason, communities which have an Internet presence are both local and global.

This local/global dimension should be an encouragement to the churches to experiment with the Internet in a creative way. At present, most church Internet involvement is in the provision of information databases or designed as a form of supplementary electronic notice boards. If the churches are to realise the potential of the Internet truly to strengthen community they will have to put more resources and imagination into making their Web sites real opportunities for communication. They need to be educationally and personally involving. They should encourage real social interaction. This is not to suggest that there should be an explosion of cyberchurches or virtual dioceses. Rather it is to suggest that the Internet should be treated as a communication domain in its own right that needs to develop its own creative repertoire.

There are more and more people, at all levels, who are trying to exploit the Internet in imaginative ways. They need to be encouraged and emulated. To take just one very simple example, Teddington Baptist Church offers the visitor to its Web site (http://ourworld.compuserve.com/homepages/cphicks/tbchome.htm) a "Virtual Baptist Church Tour". Of course, the idea is not new and there are probably thousands of more technically sophisticated "tours" on jazzier Web sites. But, compared to many other Web pages hosted by local churches, this site shows a willingness to try to exploit the strengths of the Internet in order to really communicate with the visitor to its pages.

The churches should be at the forefront of those who are demanding that people be alerted to the social, cultural, political and ethical implications of the Internet and of information technologies generally. This is not the place to spell out those implications, but no discussion of church involvement with the Internet should ignore them. In relation to the development of communities in particular, the churches have an important role to play in helping to ensure that poorer communities and individuals in the "real world" are not further disadvantaged by exclusion from, or allowed limited access to, the "virtual world" of the Internet. In this aim they have many natural allies among those groups, such as UK Communities Online, which are working to create a public space on the Internet in which all communities and sections of the community can find a way to share in the benefits of information technology.

Finally, the churches should have a strong commitment to the promotion of "Internet literacy". Those who fear that we are creating a world in which intellectual and moral discrimination will disappear in an ocean of information have a responsibility to help people find ways to navigate that ocean successfully. The uncharted waters of the Internet need to be explored and charted. In the preoccupation with the sea monsters of pornography and cults, churches and other groups are neglecting to teach the navigational skills that will help people discover, use and evaluate the hypertext routes that will be intellectually and imaginatively enriching. Communities on and off the Internet need people with such skills if they are to ensure that this new technology is truly a technology that will serve the common good. Above all, the aim should be to strengthen the possibilities for real communication and interaction between people. Only in so far as the Internet is a true medium of communication will it be a true medium for the building of communities.

Dr Jim McDonnell is director of the Catholic Communications Centre, London.

Chapter Five

One for all: Exclusion and exclusiveness

by Catherine Shelley

We are now beginning to see a far greater assimilation of faith communities within the mainstream of social and political change. There are increasing numbers from non-Christian faith communities involved in local politics, and now a member of the Muslim community in Parliament. It is a small start, but it is a sure sign of the gradual progress towards increased visibility of members of faith communities within our public life.

The fact that different parts of a community may assimilate at different rates and stages means that different forms and ways of working may develop between different groups within faith communities. At one end of the spectrum are those whose concerns are about religious discrimination, whose priorities will be the recognition of their religious festivals and space for religious observances. This may be disappointing for those who want to involve minority faith communities in anti-poverty campaigns. At the other end are those – often from the "black-led" churches – who are only too aware from their own communities of the injustices of unemployment, discrimination and racial violence. These are groups of people who want to take their part in society but are forced on to the margins by discrimination and poverty. Such communities are exasperated by the mainstream churches' lack of urgency in dealing with such issues.

The fact that matters of faith and religion are largely seen as personal and private is a large part of the reason why faith communities, and their role in society, have been overlooked by policy makers. There is, in some quarters, sensitivity about this, a fear of the possible use of resources and position for proselytising. However, most of the time it is simply oversight, and even ignorance, which forgets about faith communities. An example of this was one local authority community development project in which a group had already begun to work in a particular ward of the town. A working group had been gathered from a range of agencies and community groups in the area and had got the community-oriented Anglican church on board. The project workers had not, however, thought about any other faith communities. Once they had their eyes opened to this dimension of their community, they suddenly realised that they had seven different faith traditions on their doorstep.

Part of the problem is that, in most political wards, there is an Anglican church, with a vicar who will generally be from the UK, with all that means in terms of understanding the culture – local politics, mayoral pomp and circumstance, etc. But there are far fewer ministers of religion within other faith communities, so they will tend to be less visible and, therefore, less involved. The lower visibility arises from a number of factors.

First, there are less of these ministers, and therefore, at a very practical level, far fewer to go round all the varieties of possible forums and meetings. Their focus will tend to be ministry to their own community, which may be more pastorally demanding – because of immigration issues, unemployment, low income, etc – than many predominantly white congregations.

Second, these faith communities are less visible in architectural terms, with only a few community buildings by comparison with the Anglican church on each corner. Nor do other faith communities have the presence of their own community schools as a structural witness to their existence. They are also less obvious in national life, in that it is the Anglican church that tends to have the personnel and resources to take on chaplaincy posts in the public sector – for example, in hospitals and prisons – or formal chaplaincy posts – for example, chaplain to the mayor. At national level, there are of course the differences of profile due to Anglican establishment, such as Bishops in the House of Lords, the faith of the monarch and, therefore, the profile of St Paul's Cathedral and Westminster Abbey at moments of national celebration or mourning.

By force of circumstances and pressure of ministry to their own community, many religious leaders tend to have a lower public profile than their Anglican counterparts. In many cases, leaders of non-Christian faith communities are also not originally from the UK. This may put them at a disadvantage in dealing with the structures and processes of UK society, in terms both of knowledge of the culture and of the processes for getting things done in the UK.

But the differences of profile are not simply due to circumstance, background and pressure of work. Theologically speaking, there are also differences, in that the Anglican church will see itself as being there for the whole community as its parish, while minority faith communities – Christian and otherwise – would tend to see their parish or community entirely as those who are actively signed up to its membership in some way or other.

A further theological difference for some communities will also be that their understanding of what they are about is that they are withdrawn from "the world" – be they Buddhist communities, or Jehovah's Witnesses, or an enclosed Catholic order. For the most part, however, there will be some degree of wanting to engage with the wider community, whether simply to counteract discrimination and tackle problems for members of their own communities, or to tackle wider issues of social justice.

What seems to have led to positive examples of working together, both in an ecumenical and an inter-faith context, is building on common areas of interest and expertise, rather than just theological dialogue or disagreements about doctrine. Experience suggests that it is in doing theology, and building relationships, that the community of the kingdom is best built.

Rather than dividing, theology and spirituality could, and should, unite different faith communities. It is the first common point of interest between such communities that they hold beliefs in a transcendent dimension to life, a perspective which values the activities and achievements of the material world, but which puts them into a different, an eternal, context and perspective. It is a more explicit acknowledgement of questions about purpose and meaning in life, the universe and everything than is generally considered by those operating on a non-faith basis. That is not to say that secular humanists and atheists are not concerned with matters of morality, meaning of life or meaning which leads to social action, but there is a significant difference of perspective.

Where questions of faith come most strongly into operation is in the area of pastoral practice, particularly at times of illness and death. This means that areas of work in the community, such as hospital chaplaincy, are vitally important. It is where people are most likely to consider pure faith questions. The increasing pressure on hospital staff means that there is a tendency to forget about the chaplain(s), not to ask the question about a patient's faith background or whether they want to see a chaplain. Yet, at a time of crisis, a good chaplain can make a major difference to someone who is in pain and perhaps in fear of dying. The same goes for relatives, too.

The general rule is that the chaplaincy service in a hospital trust will be co-ordinated by an Anglican priest. Where it is run properly, he or she will have good links with the other ministers of faith in the area, ensuring that they are recognised as such and given the help they need to carry out their ministry. An effectively co-ordinated team of chaplains can bring a solidarity and comprehensiveness to the service, which means that problems such as failures to notify patients of their presence can be addressed together. The presence of chaplains of other faith communities may also allow questions of religious sensitivity and practice – for example, diet, prayer spaces, etc – to be taken up formally, and more expeditiously, with the hospital authorities. A further dimension of faith and health is the importance of religious beliefs, attitudes and anxieties in assessing a patient's state of mental health.

Similar considerations may apply in the case of death, and where funerals need to be arranged. A good example of the way in which the Church of England is used as the benchmark in a number of situations is the process used to draw up figures for DSS funeral payments. Many of the funeral service expenses were drawn from the Anglican Church's standard stipends. While there was consultation within the wider community, most of those who responded were not from the faith communities. The time given to respond to such consultations means that it is rare that they could get on to the agenda of the Inner Cities Religious Council (ICRC). Yet it is in precisely such circumstances that respect for differences between faith communities and their religious practices can have a major social consequence, and be recognised as issues which are fundamental to human dignity. To simply take figures from the Anglican Church's practice is not good enough.

Outside the mainstream church and political networks – such as the ICRC, the Standing Advisory Committee on Religious Education (SACRE) and hospital chaplaincies – there are many examples of informal networks of Interfaith activity. Most major cities, particularly those with large ethnic minority communities, have some form of interfaith network, with retreats, public meetings and campaigning activities. Good examples, among many, are Westminster Interfaith, Faith in Leeds, Faith in Bradford and Brighton's Interfaith Forum. All too often, though, such groups are seen as being on the fringe of the churches' main activities. They rely mostly on voluntary contributions and fragile personal contacts.

A more established movement which brings faith communities and many others together is Broad-Based Organising. Unlike the Interfaith networks, Broad-Based is not specifically aimed at faith-based links. It aims to bring together all parts of the community in a common aim – whether that be holding politicians to account, seeking change from a local business, or, as in the example of the East London Broad-Based organisation, TELCO, campaigning for a mosque.

The difference between the Interfaith networks and Broad-Based Organising is that the latter brings together people working in partnership from across the whole community. As it is an external organisation which facilitates the process of working together, rather than one of the faith communities themselves, there can be a greater degree of equality in developing an agenda and setting priorities than when a particular section of the community leads the process.

Other examples of working together are campaigns and movements which bring together people from a range of communities, faith-based and otherwise, around specific political issues – such as asylum and deportation. There would probably be scope for similar action around other issues in time.

Working as a community with one set of beliefs, and a particular membership, within and alongside other communities, can cause tensions between holding on to a sense of identity as a faith community and being open to God in the needs and activities of those outside the community. The Anglican approach to community, which accepts as a potential parishioner anyone living within the parochial boundaries, is the most inclusive of all. It is an approach derived largely from their political role as the established church, as much as from a necessary theology.

Such an approach has an admirable breadth of inclusiveness,

but it is not without its problems. One problem is that the inclusiveness can be misleading. For example, although obliged to marry within the parish boundaries, this does not apply if it is a marriage outside the church's law – for example, a second marriage after a divorce is generally not permissible. Similarly, communion can be given only to those in good standing with their own church. This slightly gives the lie to those who claim all within the area of a parish as their parishioners.

It also causes some grief to those of other communities who do not want to be considered as an Anglican parishioner, but to be recognised as a member of an equal faith community (or, for atheists, of none). This is particularly so in areas where those of other faiths are in the majority. The current system and Establishment perpetuates the Anglican Church's predominant position as the most powerful faith community, despite the fact that in many places it may have smaller numbers attending and actively involved in the church than other faith communities.

It is unclear, however, whether simply disestablishing the Church of England will change this predominance significantly, at least in the short term. There are too many other factors within the English establishment and culture – not least the greater number of churches and full-time personnel – which will perpetuate the pre-eminence of the established church. Inertia means that the historical presence of churches and church-related charitable funds will be preserved far longer than the numbers at services might suggest. This is not a problem so long as it is recognised and handled sensitively.

For other faith communities, their perception of their role is as being there for their own, for those who are signed up in some way as members – whether through baptism, other initiation ceremony, cultural mores or, as in the case of Jews and Hindus, through race. There is a need for a degree of exclusivity to preserve a sense of communal and cultural identity, to maintain the distinctiveness of what is taught and what the faith and its community is about. This was particularly the case for those in the earlier generations of immigration, and it can make working with other communities and the wider community quite threatening, at least initially. For vulnerable communities, integration can be a major threat.

Again, there are different theologies at work, and in all faith communities, members can be found at different degrees of assimilation and collaboration. The essence of these theological strands is how a community sees its faith, vis-à-vis the surrounding culture. One of the most noted Christian theologians to write about this was Reinhold Niebuhr, who discerned four different approaches to the search for God and truth within the surrounding or prevailing culture.

First, there is the total withdrawal from the world to find God, either in total solitude as a hermit or simply in enclosed communities of entirely the same philosophical view – for example, enclosed religious orders in the Christian tradition, the Hasidic Jews in the Stamford Hill area of north London, or enclosed communities in Buddhist monasteries. There is a total independence from the norms and expectations of the wider society in terms of getting work in the community, payment of taxes, etc. God is only to be found in the pure practice of the faith in an isolated, totally faith-centred environment.

The next stage is a strong sense of being counter-cultural, of not subscribing to the prevailing norms, of wanting to live in ways which are distinctive from those norms, yet not removed from the world entirely. An example might be the approach of the Jehovah's Witness, who will not participate in political and other structures of society, deeming them to be not of God. However, these groups, despite following their own norms, will integrate in society to the extent of taking work and participating in the economic life of the community. There is a strong sense of counter-culture and wanting to convert the rest of the world to God's way.

The third stage is a strong sense of community and the desire to maintain a sense of community identity – through, for example, limiting marriage out of the tradition. Yet there is an integration with wider society in most respects, seeking work, involvement in political and economic structures, with a view to bringing the insights and witness of faith and God to the wider community and society's structures. It is counter-cultural to the degree that some values may not accord with the prevailing culture, but much of the prevailing culture is accepted; those bits which are not accepted are to be reformed. An example might be the Catholic Church and its views on life issues, from abortion to euthanasia. In this model, God is at work in the world, but largely through the revealed truth and witness of the faith community in question.

A final, distinct stage is that which might be styled the liberal approach, under which God is being continually revealed at work in the world and the signs of the times. The prevailing culture is good and God's work can be discerned in the activities of all sections of the community. It is for the community of the faithful to discern what is good, and of God, in the world about them, and to make known the signs of God's hope in the events of this world. It is an approach seen in the Catholic Church's teaching in documents such as "Nostra Aetate", the main document on interfaith collaboration, exhorting working alongside "all people of goodwill", and "Gaudium et Spes", which explicitly states that "the joys and hopes, sorrows and fears" of the world are matters of concern to the Christian faithful.

The latter two approaches are much more likely to be amenable to working with other groups, whether other faith communities or secular groups. The chances are that, within any faith community, there will be people operating out of different perceptions along this spectrum of embracing the culture or distancing oneself from it. Broadly speaking, faith community leaders, who may be the initial point of contact in most situations, will tend to be in the position of having to hold in balance tensions arising from these different perspectives. In most instances it will be the more progressive members of a community who are able to get involved in any joint activity, particularly if it has political overtones. None of this need be a barrier, but it is worth bearing in mind when developing any interfaith work as it will help understanding of where the other parties are coming from, of where their limits and boundaries may lie, and why.

Most approaches to interfaith working and collaboration tend to focus on dialogue and concerted action as their forms of exploration and witness – a necessary coming together of people-focused action, whether it is campaigning or interfaith marches. However, there may be other ways of collaborating and sharing, in terms of infrastructure and resources. For example, when buildings become a liability and a burden to maintain, it can be all too easy to forget their power for witness in the community and their value as space for the community to gather.

For many Christian congregations, particularly the older, more mainstream traditions, how to maintain and justify the maintenance of large numbers of parish churches can be a major headache. Buildings are a liability, requiring considerable investment, which becomes an increasing burden on parishioners the more the congregation decreases. Many church buildings are even more of a nightmare to maintain because of their age. This means that more effort and worry goes into maintaining churches than into mission and involvement in the wider community. This in turn can be a spur for the more impatient and mission-minded to leave the mainstream churches and start up house churches, without the burden of buildings to maintain.

Yet for many other faith communities, buildings are needed and are a luxury not owned by many groups, faith communities or otherwise. In some urban parishes, a number of imaginative schemes have seen former churches and church buildings taken over by other faith groups, whose numbers mean that they can raise the money more easily for the maintenance required. This is surely an area for very practical sharing and collaboration between faith communities. Where the church buildings can be properly adapted to become a mosque, or temple, such a transfer can serve to redress some of the misperceptions arising from the lack of architectural presence of faith communities in our towns and cities.

Gatherings and celebrations, worship and ceremony, working and learning together are crucial in developing a sense of community and identity, both of the community and as individuals within the community. Such gatherings are in themselves a form of witness, but they can also constitute an important meeting place that brings together the community, across generational and other boundaries. For many who are otherwise socially isolated, whether through illness, age, disability, unemployment or other misfortunes, a church or faith community can be a more mainstream place to meet, where you are not stigmatised or labelled as part of a "problem" group. At best, faith communities can also be powerful sources of informal care for those who need it, based on a sense of quasi-familial obligation.

Even where faith communities are at the stage of needing to preserve their identity by concentrating on supporting their own members they can have some important insights for policy makers into effective organising and building of self-help networks and projects. These may include the informal visiting and advocacy networks, educational work, and support and possible financial help for members. It is interesting to note that some of the impetus behind the UK credit union movement came from Afro-Caribbean communities with some church links. Financial help from within the Asian communities can also be important, as is the support of businesses from within a common faith community.

The importance of such insights has also begun to be appreciated on a wider scale, as shown by the recent World Bank conference set up with the specific aim of consulting faith communities about reaching out to, and working with, some of the poorer faith communities of the world in developing anti-poverty programmes.

One of the major problems with interfaith activity, just as with faith community involvement in wider society, can be fears of proselytisation. The basis for successful partnerships across the faith divide is respect for each other's position. If what is being done accords with the principles of a faith, and there is a genuine belief that God is at work in the world, then who God works through is immaterial. It is in the working together at the margins – across divisions of faith and culture, recognising that all are neighbours, whether they be Samaritan, Jew or gentile – that God's work and involvement in the world can be both discerned and revealed.

The growth of other non-Christian faith communities is also perceived as a threat to those whose perception of England is that it is a Christian country. This is perhaps exacerbated by the wish of the future monarch to be Defender of Faiths, not the Faith. It is an age-old problem of suspicion of the other. It would be strange to assume that God created the UK a Christian country. He clearly did not. Nor should it be assumed that the threat to Christianity comes from other faith communities; there is more evidence that it comes from a decline of faith altogether.

This fear of immigration on the grounds of faith also ignores the fact that many from ethnic minority communities are in fact members of a variety of Christian churches. At the same time, many who are from other faith communities were born in the UK and are, therefore, as British as their Christian or atheist neighbours. A coming together of faith communities of all ethnic backgrounds might help to make the confusion of culture and nationality a mistake of the past, and so aid a fuller recognition and understanding of some of the issues at stake.

There are clearly a number of ways in which faith communities are already working together – from informal networks and activities to official channels of representation. Whether practical responses to community building and anti-poverty work, political campaigns or the building of community and faith understanding, such work needs to be fostered. And that requires action on a number of fronts. This will include opening up existing power and resources to the benefit of a cross-community approach; making good practice, both across faith communities and within them, more widely known and appreciated; and, above all, being prepared to build relationships, overcome barriers to understanding and work together for the good of the whole community, rather than competing for converts or the predominance of a particular world view. It is in the working together for the fullness of life of all in our communities that the Kingdom is built, not in the getting of more people to a particular church or temple.

Catherine Shelley was the first Parliamentary officer for Church Acion on Poverty, editor of the *Christian Socialist* Magazine, and is now a Labour councillor in Brighton and Hove.

Chapter Six
At the coalface: Fighting deprivation

by Paulette Haughton

When Jesus said, "The poor will always be with you", was this a promise, a prediction or a sociological statement? The church, at various times, has interpreted the words of Christ in all these ways. Within most religions there is a tradition of being kind to those on the edges of society. Christianity often treats the poor and socially excluded as a necessary evil – necessary for the church to prove that it is carrying out its mission. After all, there must be someone to help, and it is more blessed to give than to receive. It could be said that it is in the best interests of the church to ensure that there are always recipients of its largesse.

The *Faith in the City* report of 1985, commissioned by the then Archbishop of Canterbury, Lord Runcie, tackled the question of how the church could and should respond to poverty, disadvantage and marginalisation. It helped to put poverty on the map as a phenomenon that is happening at home – no longer just a distant experience in the Third World. This was no cosy theologising in the comfort of the bishops' palaces. The Church of England, and many others with it, saw the opportunity and the duty to deploy some resources in the practical outreaching of their mission to "love thy neighbour". The Church Urban Fund has proved to be one of the most effective of the Faith in the City recommendations implemented, in terms of its continuing challenge to urban deprivation, to individuals and organisations across the board. It looks poverty in the face and challenges people to ask: "What would Christ have done?"

But social exclusion, of the scale and nature we observe today, is relatively new. Certainly, there have been groups and communities throughout history that were viewed as treated as outsiders – from lepers, to Protestants, to people with Aids, prostitutes, African slaves, blacks, Jews, gentiles, travellers, from aristocrats to the poor. Most of these examples were in some way united through a shared history or experience, which directly

75

led to their exclusion. They previously had a shared or group identity that melded them together, and so they were not automatically fragmented and made powerless through the insidious process of social exclusion.

Social exclusion can start early in life. Exclusion from school and social exclusion are clearly related phenomena, and both are on the increase in our society, providing fodder for the expanding "exclusion industry". The links between unemployment and crime have long been debated, and many individuals serving time at Her Majesty's Pleasure were unemployed just before their incarceration. The connection between unemployment and imprisonment is clear, but the causal relationship is less so. Links between young people who have been in the care of local authority social services departments and those in prison are well documented. Low educational achievement, an absentee parent, being from a visible minority group and living in the inner city are also common features of excluded individuals, groups and communities.

Faith in the City declared: "Poverty is not about shortage of money. It is about rights and relationships; about how people are treated and how they regard themselves; about powerlessness, exclusion and loss of dignity. Yet the lack of an adequate income is at its heart." In a book called *The Dispossessed*, Robert Wilson and Donovan Wylie wrote: "Poverty is not difficult to define. Poverty is a state of want or deprivation that gravely interferes with someone's life. Those who want to work but can't; those who want to feed their families adequately but can't; those who want to clothe themselves and their children decently but can't; those who want to live in habitable housing conditions but can't; those who want to educate themselves or their children but can't; those whose lives are made smaller by the lack of money. These people are poor. They're poor. That's what they are."

The poor are always somehow seen as "other"; they are never ourselves or part of us. Until we – religious establishment and individual citizens – begin to be inclusive in our attitude towards our colleagues, associates, neighbours, poverty will always result in exclusion.

Unemployment can generate poverty, but unemployment and poverty do not lead inexorably to social exclusion. While some impoverished groups remain on the edges of, but still "this side" of, social exclusion, there is a level of poverty that is characterised by generations of family members lacking adequate education, employment, housing and income. The resulting loss of dignity, lack of confidence and absence of choices in life become part of a circle that is difficult to penetrate. This latter group, with its cyclical and endemic poverty, may be the people to whom Jesus referred when he said, "the poor will always be with you". The church needs to address the cyclical nature of poverty and the relevance and effectiveness of its interventions.

The nature of poverty has changed and is changing, as is the nature and the place of work. There was a time, maybe apocryphal, when people said: "We were poor but happy. There was always love in our family." The poverty at that mythical time was of a financial nature. Today, the poverty that pervades western society seems to be deeper than merely monetary and material. There is a very real and worrying poverty of soul; spiritual and moral deprivation is a growing phenomenon. This type of poverty is probably more widespread among those who have material wealth; it is prevalent among politicians, industrialists, entrepreneurs, those who run multinational corporations. This moral bankruptcy among the powerful decision-makers is dangerous and damaging; it contributes greatly to the financial poverty of the socially excluded. The church needs to find an adequate response to this type of poverty as well. While practical measures to alleviate the immediate distress caused by unemployment and material deprivation are required urgently, it is also essential that the church is more proactive in forging partnerships with powerful secular institutions to identify and address the root causes of both material and spiritual poverty.

Across the planet, the poor outnumber the privileged. In some areas of the British Isles, the poor and socially excluded will very soon be in the majority. Powerlessness often goes hand in hand with unemployment and poverty. Part of the role of the church, for individual members, churches and the corporate church, is to give a voice to the silent and to enable power to be used in creative ways that do not involve money. But part of the role of the church is also to present choices to the excluded. Education, information, knowledge are there for the taking; the church can enable individuals and groups to make choices about what is important, to prioritise and to look at an alternative future than the one that seems inevitable

In considering the position of the church, vis-à-vis work, there is the Judeo-Christian view of work and social inclusion. My father used to say to us as children: "If you don't work, you can't eat." This essentially sums up the Judeo-Christian attitude to employment. Gainful employment is the means through which individuals validate their existence. In common with most children, we were expected to help out around the home, but unlike many children we were never in any serious danger of food being withheld if we were unproductive.

Throughout Christianity, work has been of vital importance in validating the individual and, sometimes, in ensuring a place in the hereafter. Work, either paid or unremunerated, is a central theme through the Bible. Right from the beginning, in Genesis, mankind was given one rest day and the other six days for work. Christ encouraged His followers to "work, for the night is coming". He told a number of parables that emphasised the place of labour and the fairness of a day's pay for a day's work.

In the Bible, as today, individuals were identified by their occupations. David, before he put on his royal crown, worked as a shepherd and sometime harpist; St Paul made tents; St Luke was a physician, St Matthew at one time worked for the Roman treasury. And so the list goes on. Christ Himself was a carpenter. We still identify and locate people by their profession or job – and, to a lesser extent, by their family connections. When meeting someone new, one of the first questions is: "So what do you do for a living?" If talking about a friend's new partner, most people will inquire fairly early in the discussion what he or she "does".

In the Judeo-Christian tradition, work has always been important in order to have the means with which to contribute to the religious community. There are priests to support, ministries to develop, places of worship to be built and the poor to be fed and clothed. Therefore, if someone was not working, not gainfully employed, they were unable to participate in the activities of the community and thus became an outsider, one of the socially excluded and financially dependent.

Most churches are conservative, conventional, law-abiding institutions, with congregations to match. Church members believe that work is an activity sanctioned by God; therefore, all able-bodied individuals of sound mind owe it to the Creator to be active and industrious members of their society. Work, labour, gainful employment, whatever it is called, the activity in which an individual sells his or her time and expertise is seen as a God-given activity. It is respectable to work and degrading to be out of work for any extended period of time. People gain their self-respect through work, and the Church supports this attitude.

The Church has always recognised that there will be people who, for whatever reason, are unable to work and therefore need to be supported. The level and nature of financial support and help-in-kind given by the Church has, traditionally, shied away from encouraging dependence. There is a lingering notion of the deserving and undeserving poor – those who, through no fault of their own, are in need, as opposed to the drunks and wastrels of life. It is probably politically unsound for the church to differentiate, but an uneasy feeling lingers that most religious institutions maintain some formal or informal hierarchy of help-worthiness.

The phenomenon that we call social exclusion is linked to selfishness and a lack of social responsibility and conscience. Many would call it wickedness, but others make a slightly more quantifiable analysis: the effects of 18 years of Conservative governments, Thatcherism and the effects of profit-at-all-costs, the free market economy and the attendant unemployment. The resulting economic divergence – prosperity for some and decline for many – has continued, with far more people becoming poor than becoming rich. Social exclusion and poverty are issues that will continue to hold interest and to raise concern because the victims of poverty are not just the unwashed masses; the respectable middle classes can foresee a time when they may also be poor.

All attempts that government and other social institutions are making to address issues of exclusion and poverty are to reassure the middle classes that they will not suffer the fate of the poor and excluded of today. The Church is not so cynical; it acts from a principled stand rather than one of naked self-interest. Unemployed and, because of the education system, unemployable, growing numbers pushed out of society are now seeing no place for themselves. Notions of citizenship are almost obsolete among such people.

The Church is not very visible. It is entirely possible that people are doing things in a low-key way, keeping the left hand from knowing what the right is doing. Many churches are inward looking, perhaps offering help and assistance within their own membership and not reaching out. Those that do reach out do so in a quiet, unassuming way. Should the Church be more visible? Should it work in partnership with secular organisations to relieve poverty?

Across the country, the Church is dying; its membership is elderly white people and urban black families. Of course, this is something of an overstatement, but in London, for example, the thriving churches have largely African and Caribbean congregations. Some of the same people who are perceived as being socially excluded are the same people who join churches, seeking both human and divine support. The irony of this situation is clear: the disenfranchised, poor and socially excluded join an organisation having as one of its central tenets the concern for and care of the poor.

A number of urban churches have outreach programmes – the poor reaching out to the poor. Inner-city congregations see need, powerlessness and deprivation both inside and outside the church. A number of denominations, including the Seventh-Day Adventists and Church of God, have prison visiting programmes, and they organise crèches, mother and toddler groups, drop-in sessions for the lonely and out of work, youth clubs and food distribution for the homeless, among other activities. Individual churches are running numerous programmes across the country; the thing they have in common is that, in the main, they are independent of the corporate church. Local action by local communities, sometimes within their own neighbourhoods, and at other times acting on behalf of people considered to be more disadvantaged than them. It is a syndrome that can be observed on any main street of our cities: the least well-dressed person gives money to casual beggars, while the materially wealthy, but "poor in spirit", cross by on the other side of the road.

Since May 1997, Welfare to Work and the New Deal for the unemployed has been the government's answer to long-term unemployment among those aged 18 to 24 years. The thinking behind the scheme is sound: to counsel and train people and give them real jobs with adequate wages. This will go a long way towards self-reliance and will encourage people to develop and influence their own destiny. But the implementation of

Welfare to Work in the current economic and employment scene is flawed: there are not enough jobs of the kind that are needed. In addition, the use of penalties and the lack of choice are not appropriate measures in the operation of such a scheme. The government, through the employment service, provides subsidies for employers and voluntary organisations that are willing to provide placements for the unemployed client.

Has the Church a role to play in Welfare to Work? How many Church-based organisations are geared up to providing placements for young people? Should the Church be involved in such a scheme? The Church will have to take a stand on these issues, especially when the scheme is expanded to take account of the long-term unemployment among people over 25, single parents and people with disabilities.

A number of locally-based programmes have been started as a result of growing concern at the number of young men and boys who either were not in school or had no jobs. Welfare to Work provided a further opportunity to engage the young people in more productive avenues. This picture is repeated across London, and in cities like Birmingham, Bradford and Leeds. Indeed, the Church Urban Fund supports a number of employment-related projects, some of which will be actively engaging the provisions of Welfare to Work.

But most religions are holistic philosophies and seek to be relevant to all aspects of the lives of their followers. Some religions reach outside of their communities in ways that do not attempt to convert people. As a major world religion, Islam involves itself in a wide range of activities to support the needy in its ranks. The Regent's Park mosque in central London seemed to be a good place to find out about Islamic involvement in community measures and, specifically, about moves to combat social exclusion within the Islamic communities. A spokesman told me that he "wouldn't be surprised if there was nothing. Muslims are just beginning to emerge as a settled community, we are just about to assert a Muslim identity." But he suggested longer established Muslim communities, such as those in Bradford and Birmingham, may be responding to powerlessness and social exclusion.

Membership of the Nation of Islam is growing rapidly among young people of African origin. The picture in North America is being reflected in our inner cities here in the UK: members are being drawn from existing Christian congregations and, like Malcolm X, from those with a Christian upbringing. Recruitment is especially successful among the most marginalised and angry young people, especially those in prison. While perceived by the mainstream as being poor and disadvantaged, many individuals do not accept this definition, preferring to see themselves as living in a parallel existence. Part of the success of Islam in recruiting converts is that it takes people from social exclusion to religious inclusion. This sense of belonging can actually remove the impetus towards a more general form of social inclusion.

There is a sense in which people from visible minorities in Britain allow themselves to be excluded from civic life by clinging to the belief that some day they will "go home". The home they are speaking about is terrestrial, rather than celestial. It is time second and third generation representatives of these minorities accepted that this green and pleasant land is home. The internalisation of the role of outsider allows the label of excluded to become part of the identity of both individual and community. This is not to deny the effects of endemic and institutionalised racism on poverty, unemployment and exclusion; once this has been acknowledged, the fight for inclusion must include an acceptance of the roles and responsibilities of citizens, and not only the rights of settlers.

Visible minorities, who comprise a large percentage of the socially excluded in the cities, are not similarly represented in rural areas, where poverty is of a different, but equally soul-destroying, nature. Rural poverty among the indigenous population is an issue that government, charitable trusts and the corporate church are starting to recognise. But recognition and action are, in the main, still strangers to each other.

The Church has a role to play in removing distinctions between "them" and "us". Those labelled as socially excluded can be seen as evidence that the Church has failed to have an inclusive ministry, both at a theological and at a practical level. How many vicars are from the same social background as their inner-city parishioners? In truth, this should not prevent communication and empathy – both areas the Church must improve upon. Can the Church really hope to reach the socially excluded, the unemployed and the poor when there is such a yawning gap between their needs and wants and what the

Church has to offer? Involvement is essential when trying to engage and include people. A first step would be for the Church to involve, actively and realistically, those on the outside, to work with them rather than solely for them.

The Church, as a corporate body, is strangely inactive and largely silent on the demise of work and subsequent escalation of poverty and lack of inclusiveness. Individual churches are all too well aware of the effects of poverty and unemployment both on their members and on the wider neighbourhood and localities.

The mission of the Church is an earthly one with a heavenly objective. Even if people in need are interested only in an improved level of existence in this life, it is incumbent on the church to help in as many arenas and in as any ways as is required. The founder of Christianity talked, socialised with, comforted and helped all those who needed His assistance. He challenged the comfortable to respond to the comfortless. The institutions His followers have set up must aim to do no less.

So where does power lie? Power and decision-making are being removed from communities and localities. The place of the Church in local politics has been taken over by the local council. Often local government may be more representative of local interests, but commonly is not as concerned over local needs. The power of the global marketplace determines local life. Superstores replace the corner shop, unwanted roads are built to cope with increased commercial traffic, post offices are shut down, and so on. Power is no longer in local hands. In addition to the disempowerment of the individual, people have become consumers and customers rather than citizens. Many people no longer participate in civic life; turnouts at election time are steadily falling because "it doesn't make a difference". True powerlessness is the absence of choice, and choices are rapidly being eroded.

Is there any sense in which people accept exclusion as a way of life? Do they surrender their personal, God-given equality and personal power? Each individual has the power to forgive, to question, to love, to learn, to teach and to share. The phenomenon that is social exclusion results in the individual abrogating these basic rights: the Church must assist and encourage individuals and groups to regain their humanity and to recognise their self-worth. Too often the Church provides first aid, rather than seeking to empower individuals and communities. It does not routinely become engaged with government – local, regional or national. On the occasions that it does, there is always criticism and loud calls for the separation of Church and state. There have been, and still are, exceptions, such as the national Coalfields Churches Conference, convened jointly in 1993 by the Industrial Mission in South Yorkshire, Church Action on Poverty, the Coalfields Chaplains Network and the Diocese of Sheffield Social Responsibility Committee. The local knowledge and the understanding of the implications of pit closures on local people directed the churches into action. Even though the closures went ahead, the church had discovered a renewed political context for its ministry.

The Church – or, more accurately, certain sections of it – has always considered Christianity to be a practical, positive and participatory philosophy, and not simply a personal spiritual exercise. We have referred to the Jewish principle of taking care of the weak and vulnerable within their faith; this is common among religions. First, you take care of your own – the weak, vulnerable and excluded people within your community. Only then is it appropriate to go outside.

According to the Council of Churches for Britain, "churches themselves are deeply involved in the world of work and with the social issues that have been the concern of our inquiry . . . the Catholic Young Christian Workers, the Social Responsibility Boards, the Justice and Peace Committees, the William Temple Foundation, the Industry Churches' Forum, the Von Hugel Institute, and too many more to list." We could add the admirable St Vincentians to this list. Their mission statement sums up one of the main roles of the church: "The Society collaborates with other people of good will in relieving need and addressing its causes, making no distinction in those served, because in them Vincentians see the face of Christ."

The Church runs a good number of employment projects. The Peckham Evangelical Churches' Action Network (PECAN) in south London is a good example of a Christian-based employment programme. Set up around the time of the *Faith in the Cities* report in the late 1980s, PECAN responded to a skills shortage in an area of high unemployment. Official figures and local estimates gave the figures as between 30 and 50 per cent male unemployment in the area, though there are claims that this figure has fallen in the past 12 months. Not satisfied with inviting the unemployed to come to them, PECAN adopted the method of knocking on doors and seeking out people. It now trains more than 1,600 local residents a year and has a total annual turnover of more than £100,000, of which the bulk is from statutory grants; PECAN also accesses resources from a range of central government initiatives.

PECAN is an example of a joint initiative across denominations. More common are the small, local projects set up by local people; one such project is based at the St Matthew's Methodist church in East London. Run by young men from Bow, mostly black, mostly graduates, it started with a youth club. The project has expanded to offer work-related training, advice and support and to encourage local regeneration and sustainable development in the area. PECAN co-operates with the Employment Service, local employers, community members and church members.

Jubilee 2000 represents a different level of church intervention, attempting to deal with a global problem of systemic poverty and social and economic inequity. Based on the Biblical notion of Jubilee – the periodic cancelling of debt and celebration of justice – Jubilee 2000 has petitioned the leaders of the major industrialised nations to initiate a one-off cancellation of the backlog of unpayable poor country debts in the year 2000. It also proposes the development of a proper plan to avoid the further build up of unpayable debt after the start of the new millennium. Jubilee 2000 is a campaign initiated by church movements, but has worked in partnership with social activists, politicians and the private enterprise sector, as well as individuals. The campaign has moved beyond the more traditional church responses to poverty, referred to earlier, and engages in energetic, multi-faceted political and social action to eradicate a root cause of poverty in many of the world's poorest countries. The campaign can justifiably claim a positive impact on the policies of inter-governmental and international organisations dealing with third world debt.

The modern day Church tries to treat the socially excluded as deserving of its charity, unless the position as social outcast is perceived as being of the individual's own making. Some Christian denominations imply that deliberate sinners cannot be helped until they have repented, hence groups such as homosexuals are excluded because they are wilful sinners reaping the consequences of their actions, and therefore completely beyond the pale. Sexual immorality creates excluded groups within Christianity – more so than in the secular world, where the socially excluded are more often characterised by material poverty, by cultural and educational deficiencies, rather than moral and spiritual deficiencies.

A few years ago, poverty was not an acceptable word in most political circles. There was certainly "no poverty" in England. When a number of charities, such as Oxfam and the Peabody Trust, made it clear that poverty was a feature not only of the developing world, but also of the industrialised nations, they were castigated for the very suggestion. Today, nobody bats an eyelid when the National Lottery Charities Board lists alleviation of poverty as one of its causes. It is accepted that poverty exists in the UK.

Although still the wealthiest city in the country, London is also home to 14 of the 20 poorest wards in England. Some 60 per cent of the young people going to Centrepoint, a large homelessness charity based in London's West End, are not outsiders attracted to the city by the lure of employment and fast money, but young Londoners who have fallen through every social net. An increasing proportion of the capital's homeless people come from within London itself. Young people leaving the care of local authorities are disproportionately represented among single homeless people, and there is also a worrying over-representation of people from black and minority ethnic communities.

In a number of key areas, the report points to a startling divergence between the poorest and the wealthiest. For example, the life expectancy of the poor has dropped, while the wealthy can expect to live longer and healthier lives than ever before. Material poverty caused by unemployment and underemployment has resulted in greater numbers of people living on the fringes of, if not outside, mainstream society.

When it comes to defining poverty and social exclusion, the London Borough of Southwark says helpfully: "Social exclusion is the denial, or non take-up, of social rights, by individuals and groups because of their poverty, lack of power, alienation and experience of discrimination. Social rights includes access to goods and services, involvement in local and general elections, knowledge of rights and the ability to influence the existing power structure and decision makers."

The Seventh-Day Adventist church I attend in south London organises food distribution to homeless people in the centre of London. It is not alone. Many local churches see feeding the homeless as a way of responding to Christ's instruction to "clothe the naked and feed the hungry". It is difficult to fault the motives behind the feeding, if not of the 5,000, of men and women who live in cardboard boxes and move from doorway to embankment as the weather dictates. But is this simply "giving the man a fish, rather than teaching him to fish for himself"? Are there more effective ways of responding to social exclusion than dealing with the apparent symptoms? How should the Church tackle the root causes of poverty, unemployment and exclusion? Could it be that such palliative measures are to soothe the consciences of the members, rather than to ease the suffering of the homeless?

Paulette Haughton is director of Kenté, a voluntary organisation which works with ethnic minority organisations in the London area.

Selected reading
Hilary Russell, *Poverty Close to Home* (Mowbray, 1995).
Michael Northcott (Editor), *Urban Theology: A Reader* (Cassell, 1998).
Strengthening Communities (Church Urban Fund annual review, 1996).
Barriers: Social and Economic Exclusion in London (London Voluntary Service Council, 1998).
Inquiry into Poverty in Four London Boroughs (City Parochial Foundation, June 1995; unpublished).

Chapter Seven
Mixed blessings: Suburban experiences
by Pen Wilcock

"He also said, 'This is what the Kingdom of God is like. A man throws seed on the land. Night and day, while he sleeps, when he is awake, the seed is sprouting and growing; how, he does not know. Of its own accord the land produces first the shoot, then the ear, then the full grain in the ear. And when the crop is ready, he loses no time: he starts to reap because the harvest has come.'"

Park Road Church, in an area on the south coast of England, was the chapel where I worshipped for many years, until eventually I was trained for ordination and then became their minister for three years. Just before I trained, I wrote a book which asked the questions: "On Sunday morning, where are the black people and the people with physical disabilities? Where are the homeless people? Where are the builders' labourers? Where are the teenagers? Where are the gay people? Where are the mentally ill people and the mentally handicapped people?" My book went on to say: "I don't know where they are, but they're not in our church, or not in any significant numbers. Why not? Are there bouncers at the door to keep them out? Not at all. Everyone is welcome, or so we always say. We sit at the top of the glass mountain and we say that everyone is welcome, and we wonder why they never come." That was in 1994. Within the space of a few years, they *were* all there in our church on Sunday mornings. And this is how it happened.

Park Road Church was a Christian faith community with a reputation for flourishing youth work, for worship with a charismatic flavour, and for choosing its preachers with great care to maintain and uphold a conservative evangelical "bible-believing" approach to Christian theology. There was a mix of ages, and Sunday morning worship was culturally dominated by the presence of a band of musicians mixing violins, recorders and other traditional acoustic instruments with drums and electric guitars, plus young women singers behind an impressive row of microphones. The feel of worship was modern, passionate, exciting, and (theologically) conservative.

Church life was underpinned by the quiet input of more traditional, and in the main, elderly people. These were more cautious, less flamboyant; they were committed to their faith, wanting to learn and follow, but with less certainty about their rightness – despite the unswerving quality of their faith.

In the early 1990s, there was a crèche and Sunday school for the youngsters, and a varying number (usually two or four) of housegroups on the go. There were about three local preachers in the congregation, and a mix of types of people – professionals, manual workers, young and old. Most of the congregation was white, but not all middle class. There was also a small group with multiple disabilities from residential homes beginning to attend chapel on a Sunday morning. Initially, they sat at the back, rather nervously, but gradually gained the confidence to receive Holy Communion, for which they sat in their pews. Our minister was a gentle, unassuming man, clear in his vision for the church, but lacking in personal confidence.

Into this congregation, the Methodist Conference debate on human sexuality burst like a bombshell. At the time, I was a student minister, and a local preachers' tutor, and the seminars I held on this fraught subject caused deep trauma for the leading figures in the congregation. Outrage was deep and bitter, and many people were horrified to discover that I wished to affirm and celebrate gay sexuality, and homosexual relationships expressed in the context of permanent, faithful and stable relationships. After a turbulent period, during which I found myself unwelcome at worship in my own church and was suspended from preaching, the Methodist Conference decision to affirm and celebrate the ministry of gay men and lesbians brought the tensions to a head. About a third of the congregation left – including the treasurer, the Sunday School superintendent, most of the band, many officers, young and middle-aged adults, and most of the local preachers. The Girls' Brigade closed. The gentle minister, his confidence crushed, took early retirement.

Perhaps those least aware of this storm were the people with disabilities. They all had learning disabilities, and depended on helpers to bring them to church. In the main, their helpers were not Christian, and none of the group attended business or executive meetings, only Sunday morning worship and social gatherings. So they continued to attend church, not really aware of the enormous upheaval the rest of the community was experiencing. The community was left broken and hurt, licking its wounds and trembling with the pain of the judgment offered by those who had left us, that God, also, had left, taking his Holy Spirit with him.

The ones left behind were mainly elderly, not rich. A significant number had suffered mental illness or breakdown or chronic depression. There were very few men and few really able-bodied. We felt weak, needy and broken. Standing with the senior steward at the back of the chapel on the summer morning I began to be the minister there, the task seemed daunting, but the scene was not without humour.

We had a few babies left, who came to chapel with their mums, though rarely with their fathers. They were noisy. The disabled people were also noisy, and our congregation was not yet really used to them. We had two or three alcoholic men – dirty, dishevelled and difficult to part from their cans of lager. The scene reminded me of the story Jesus told, in which He compared the Kingdom of Heaven to a huge party, given by a king. Those invited, the dignitaries and social luminaries, had declined to be there. So the king, determined that his banquet should not be wasted, sent his servants out into the streets and the lanes to bring in whoever they could find, filling the palace with rabble until the party was complete. Park Road, that first Sunday morning, looked like that story at the point where everyone had come in and was millling around but hadn't sat down yet.

The first task was to heal the intense pain of the wound of humiliation and bereavement, and to help the people believe in themselves as a valid faith community, of sacred worth and beloved by God.

This was set in motion by a three-strand strategy. First, the existing Monday night fellowship – a small group, the remnant of the housegroup structure – became a circle of faith affirmation, in which people were invited and encouraged to tell the story of their spiritual path and spiritual experience, and to realise afresh that the Holy Spirit was present and at work in their lives, and had always been so. Eventually, we returned to Bible study and exploration of Christian themes, but the beginning was gentle, re-establishing confidence and making space for the people to be heard, to be affirmed, and to find their own agenda.

An important part of this evening meeting was the choosing and singing of hymns: they expressed the faith and choice of the individual, but without the self-exposure of expressing an opinion. This faith choice was affirmed by the group. It was a good time for those who were bewildered by the now rather chaotic experience of Sunday morning worship and it offered an experience of quiet reflection and sharing, a space to express uncertainties and grievances about the ploughing up of Park Road traditions.

Second, a programme of social and creative events was set in motion. Over the next three years, we embarked on a pantomime, a tea-dance with Palm Court orchestra, and an old-time music hall evening. Here, the purpose was to require church attenders to spend time together working on a project that stretched them, revealed their talents and abilities, and bonded them in new friendships, drawing in newcomers as the community began to grow again. Fund-raising events, such as the Christmas bazaar and the summer gift day, were also important.

People were tremendously encouraged to find that, though depleted in numbers, we had the energy and determination to surpass previous fund-raising totals – though it was done with no emphasis on raising money. The events were seen as opportunities to help, to give and to participate. We set no targets and sent no begging letters. Giving was simply thanksgiving for God's love and grace. At the general meeting the next spring, the giving of the church to others, previously frozen, was increased.

Third, I preached for a year on one theme: Everybody's Church. Sunday after Sunday I expounded a faith in the Christ who came, as Mark's Gospel has it, "not to be served, but to serve, and to give his life as a ransom for all people". The repetition of this preaching of welcome and inclusion in Christ's name began to take effect. We created an area at the back of the chapel where toddlers could have a carpet, books, toys and beanbags to feel welcome, and where they could relax. One morning, two of the helpers of our worshippers with disabilities, instead of waiting passively in the pew for Holy Communion to be brought down, lifted the wheelchair of a young man with cerebral palsy and carried him up to the rail. After that, we put a ramp in place every Sunday, and everyone came to the rail. The pews were augmented by a large, comfy armchair, for anyone who might find pews a problem.

In the spring, I put before the church council a request to take into full membership of the church our worshippers with disability. Confusion and doubt were expressed about those who could not speak or reason or communicate. The vote expressed an overwhelming weight of uncertainty. We left the issue, for the time being, with a promise of exploring it in teaching and preaching. When the council met again in the autumn, an overwhelming majority voted to receive all worshippers with learning disabilities. They had proved their commitment – getting up at 4.30am on Easter Day to be in time for the service at 8am; sending postcards when on holiday; crafting a Christmas candleholder in their day-centre workshop.

The Dover L'Arche community helped us to look at the issue of membership preparation, and on Pentecost Sunday a group of new members was admitted, those with and without disabilities all together. The key workers of those who could not speak – drawn into involvement with the faith community by a passionate concern that their friends be permitted to make the commitment which enabled them to belong – knelt beside the wheelchairs to make promises on their behalf. For those who had speech, the promises were simplified. Several received baptism, the church having, from infancy, passed them by.

When I asked the question, "Do you want to belong to Jesus in the family of this Church at Park Road?", the answer "yes!" came as an amazing shout, followed by the words of one, Peter, spoken with great dignity: "It's an honour."

In all of this, I had in mind a programme of three accessibilities, arrived at through investigations which were my responsibility as part of the Methodist Church's formation of policy about poverty at the end of the 1980s. I had discovered then that what poor people need – more than money – is the moral support of friendship, a companion on the journey, to give them the courage to find their own solutions. Church life had to express accessibility on three levels:

• Accessibility of lifestyle – we should not have homes or possessions that would shame others or tempt them either to covetousness or despair.

- Accessibility of social life – we should ensure that the Church has a rich social programme, only planning events that offer something to everyone at some level, holding out an opportunity for new talents to be explored, allowing people to shine. They should take place on an accessible premises. And they should be free.

- Accessibility of worship – disabled people should be able to get into the building, and it should be so laid out that small children feel comfortable and welcome. The songs, preaching and structuring of worship should be so designed as to be accessible to the simple and the young, but profound and challenging to the educated and sophisticated. The key to this is in story-telling, using the door of imagination, rather than intellect, in our approach to concept.

Not only were the very young, those with disabilities and the middle-aged and elderly to be made welcome, those traditionally wary of the Church needed to find a welcome too. ("Go out into the highways and byways and *compel* them to come in!")

Many people came to help us, and I think we all were enriched. Of those who came, some stayed and worshipped regularly, some became occasional worshippers, but all were blessed and became friends. And some were brought back into a gentler relationship of understanding with the Church after carrying for a long time the wounds inflicted by the unthinking hardness of dogmatic religion.

Meanwhile, aside from Sunday services, I was kept busy in the community, preparing people for marriage and baptism, taking funerals. In our church, we held that baptism was a sign of God's unconditional love, so provided that the parents (or parent) of the child showed reverence and respect for the promises they made, we turned no one away and did not impose conditions on the receiving of this sacrament of God's embrace. Most local churches laid down conditions for receiving baptism, and communication frequently broke down between clergy, who saw baptism as an initiation rite, and parents, who saw baptism from the baby's point of view as a coming to God at the start of life's journey. We welcomed them and never turned them away.

Likewise with weddings. Most local churches would marry only people who had never previously been married. We took the commitment of marriage seriously, but we accepted that things go wrong sometimes, and we offered people a chance to start again. With funerals, my practice was to start not with my belief system and ideology but from the place where the people were at. The funerals I took honoured and respected the spiritual path of the one who had died and of the bereaved; and this simple willingness to begin where they were at encouraged a better relationship with the church.

Out of these pastoral links, people began to come to Park Road Church in search of a place to belong, somewhere to bring uncertainties as well as faith, where they might live with questions, without being steam-rollered by dogma. Once in church, the people were charmed and captivated by the raggle-taggle congregation. I remember one elderly lady coming for the first time, saying that she'd never been in a church where there were so many people with something wrong with them!

Among our inquirers and regular worshippers was a sprinkling of atheists. They never found common cause with our doctrines, but they loved the Holy Spirit and, once reassured of a welcome, settled as comfortably into the community of faith as some of our staunchest supporters. And, of course, the helpers from the residential homes were not always committed to the Christian faith. They were care assistants who happened to be there. Part of the fun of preaching on a Sunday morning was the challenge of catching and keeping their interest.

In recent years, the town in which Park Road is situated has developed a wider cultural mix. It has broadened from white Anglo-Saxon, with one West Indian, to include Sierra Leonians and Finnish people, a Kenyan lady, a Chinese lady, and black British people. A strong link for the neighbourhood was the playgroup, which was not merely a letting of the premises but was part of the presence of the faith community for the area in which we were set. The playgroup was a caring, happy, thriving concern, and it ensured that about 50 young mums or other carers came through our premises with their toddlers every day of the week, forming a strong and positive interaction with the life of the church.

The chapel belonged to the neighbourhood; it was the place where they had been married, where their kids had been christened, where they held their jumble sales and where their little ones could come to playgroup. It was the place you could get coffee and biscuits on a Saturday morning.

As our life together developed and strengthened and morale rose, people became more assertive, which brought tensions as well as celebration. At first too demoralised to turn anyone away, members of the congregation turned to a more vigorous defending of their own corner as life became more settled. At any one time there would always be something simmering: little bands of old ladies muttering together, fomenting a revolution with intent to hustle out of Sunday worship into a separate room the dense crowd of tots who (with admirable, but relative, quietness) populated the children's corner; or an uprising, of those who liked worship to be quiet and decorous, against the presence of those of our members who crawled about on the floor roaring and growling or shrieking and screeching. People being what they are, sometimes the most wounding and thoughtless things were said. I had to study people management to understand the dynamic of making a diverse group work in harmony.

The church was in the early stages of cohesiveness, and my dream of an open and inclusive faith community had come to fruition, more than I had expected would be possible. But the structure was still fragile, and much work remained to be done. But by then, a reshaping of the Methodist Circuit meant a change in the staffing, and brought for me a curtailment of my stationing there and a move to another Circuit.

Underlying the work at Park Road had been the following:

- A willingness to work with directions rather than completion. This implied a willingness to meet people where they were and start at that point, without anxiety about their frequent inability to grasp some of the fundamentals of Christian faith. Faith formation doesn't happen overnight, and we live in a post-Christian age.

- A differentiation between witness and salesmanship. God can make God's own relationships with human beings and does not need us to sell the divine being like a commodity, ensuring a deal is clinched and a contract signed. It is enough to bear witness to our own experience of grace. Nothing more is necessary.

- A principle of hiddenness. We never advertised Park Road, and for a long time we could not even be found in the map or street atlas. But I relented in the end, and allowed us to have a small square giving our address and showing our location on a new map of the town. I never had any wish to drum up custom or to persuade people to come; if anything, I used to dissuade people, saying: "I don't want anyone in worship except those who really, honestly want to be there. There's no point in you coming to please me. Come if you want to come."

- A principle of unconditional grace and love. The church is not ours but God's. It is not our prerogative to set boundaries of exclusion where God has not. The boundaries of the church should be set by the discipline of loving. No one stayed the course at Park Road who was unable to accept others as they were and share the sacred space with them. Having everybody there means the congregation self-selects for tolerance – even though it gets a bit hairy at times.

- A principle of non-attachment. Practising Everybody's Church requires one to let go of attachment to being right, to success, to opinions, to structures and traditions, and to having one's own way. It also requires the acceptance of change and flux as part of life. Things ebb and flow.

- A principle of prayer and meditation. This was how our church community grew and how we maintained it.

- A principle of leadership. Like the Pied Piper, the leader needs to call the people, charm them. People will not be hectored and forced. You can't do Everybody's Church like that. But still the shepherd is not the sheep and the piper is not the child. The leader needs to understand her/his calling and wear the mantle of authority with poise and grace.

- A principle of understanding that worship is expressed in many ways, and that faith grows differently in different people. Words and doctrine can come last or never, and some of God's friends never know God by name.

After I had been minister for a while, I found the sound of my voice would settle the people to worship, though things were sometimes pretty rowdy at the start. They knew me and I think

– and hope – they knew I loved them. It has to be said that there was a certain serendipity about the way things went, but there were specific strategies as well:

- Rebuilding a sense of community by sharing our stories, and by moving very slowly, emphasising the traditions but illuminating them from within; and by setting up community projects to draw in new people and facilitate friendship bonding.

- A strong preaching ministry.

- Regular pastoral visitation of each section of the community.

- Focused prayer and meditation.

- Vigorous work in the community, especially rites of passage, over which infinite care and patience was taken.

- Planning of events, treats, things to look forward to.

- Deliberate, dogged policy of adaptability and non-arrogance.

The **Rev. Pen Wilcock** is minister for Keston and West Wickham churches in the Bromley Methodist Circuit.

Chapter Eight
Ploughing onwards: Rural experiences

by Peter Barham

In a late 1998 issue of the journal, 'Theology', Dr W.M. Jacob
wrote that the involvement of church people in the founding
of the United Nations was "so subtle that most people have
forgotten their part in it". In many ways, the involvement of
the church in rural communities is similar: past work is either
forgotten (so no one really knows what the letters CEVCP stand
for in the relation to the village school), or it is trumpeted as the
opposite of today ("When Mr Smith was Rector he ran the
cricket club."). Today, the church will still stand, perhaps the
only public building in the village, and 15 per cent of the
population of my benefice came to a harvest festival. The
community council, however, is still not keen on giving a grant
for a new PA system in the church because, it says, "more people
will use new play equipment on the green".

Let me start with the harvest festival. I'm priest-in-charge of
four villages eight miles south of the East Anglian town of Bury
St Edmunds, just north of the beautiful village of Lavenham.
Very few of the regular congregation are farmers, and many
villages have very few farmers. It seems incongruous, then, that
Betjeman's Church Mouse can comment:

> "But all the same it's strange to me
> How very full the church can be
> With people I don't see at all
> Except at Harvest Festival?"

In fact, we have found that it is necessary to have more, not
fewer, harvest festivals, and each one is different to the last – but
with the common thread of "We plough the fields and scatter".
Two villages have a Friday evening service and a ticketed harvest
supper, and the village halls burst at the seams, yet no one in the
hall has worked on anything larger than their garden for several

years now. The school comes to church for their festival, and I gently commented that none of the songs they sang us mentioned "God". For some their Sainsbury's bags of tins sit uneasily (for some) beside professional-looking floral displays. We tried Saturday harvest workshops, which worked well in the village with no school, but failed in the village with one. Then we had family services on the Sunday, which were successful in two villages, but not in the third.

We have attempted to celebrate the other agricultural festivals. Rogationtide was a beautiful day, and we walked round a large farm in the middle of the four parishes. Our route led us into all four of them, so each was blessed. We picnicked in our local nature reserve, and learnt a lot about the farm itself. Many who were with us had no idea which crop was which. When I commented on a newly-planted hedge, I was told that it was a "wildlife corridor" and that "we get grants for wildlife corridors, we don't for hedges". One farmer nearby had very overgrown footpaths and was not happy about us using them, while two of our congregation are avid walkers – which presents an interesting clash of views. People from all four parishes – including some non-churchgoers – came together, often for the first time, and walked with us, and the subsequent display of photos has whetted appetites for next year.

At my previous parish we combined Rogationtide with the centenary of the parish council. A route was planned from one end of the village to another, calling in at the apple orchard, playing field, church, pub, old people's home and village hall en route. At each point we had an appropriate Bible reading and prayer. No difficulties with the old people's home (Job 12: "Old men have wisdom, but God has wisdom and power.") or with the pub (1 Timothy 5: "Take a little wine for your health."), but the apple orchard was more of a problem. Genesis does not refer to "the apple"; the only piece is in Song of Songs – not really suitable for an all-age service!

Lammas is the service on the first Sunday in August, the first of the harvest festivals, when the first fruits are blessed. Church Services for the Farming Year, a publication of the Arthur Rank Centre, suggests meeting at a pick-your-own farm. We have one in the benefice whose owners are regular churchgoers, so we sat beside the fruit canes, plugged the keyboard into the power supply for the till (surely that's symbolic of something!), and had a short service with a congregation ranging in age from four to 90. Then we had a picnic lunch, and those who had to leave for their "proper dinner" missed the offer to "pick as much fruit as you like – free". It had been good publicity for the farm itself (some people in the benefice did not know where it was before the service), and the owners felt that their farm and their work was more valued, enjoyed and understood than before.

During the Lammas service, I commented that we had not celebrated Plough Sunday, "as it's the first Sunday in January and we don't really want to stand in the cold blessing ploughs". But one of the churchwardens did not hear that bit, and by the end of the service he had everything planned. "I'll bring my old wooden plough into church, and we can park the newer machinery in the village hall car park." How can I say "No"? Another farmer, who's just starting his own contracting business at what must be the worst possible time, commented: "I'll be there. I need all the help I can get."

My fear is that all this is a little gimmicky – and there were certainly some people who went to a "proper" Eucharist rather than a service walking round fields. But others, who could not walk, were there to see us off and to greet us back with a cup of tea. Without the support of some of the farming community the ideas would never work; with a few being keen and involved, it was worth doing. Churches are often accused of marginalising the agricultural community, or what is left of it, so perhaps this helps redress the balance. In the past, it would have been the farmers who were the bedrock of the village and the church. Now, the nearest contact most of the village has with farming is being held up behind a tractor. Perhaps the church can bridge the gap.

Every village is made up of many different communities and groups of people, as well as those who are hardly ever grouped. Many farmers seem to operate almost solely as individuals, and there are fewer and fewer opportunities for them to get together. Rogationtide and the other festivals may be an opportunity for them to be together on their terms. Often they tell you of past clergy who have lectured them at harvest festival, so now they only come to church for funerals; once that particular group of individuals has been offended, they are not willing to forgive.

In Bury St Edmunds, the cathedral hosts the annual county harvest festival, and they have had to put a great deal of effort into keeping that service going. As a county service, the "chain gang" are all there in force, and the judges, police chiefs and those you expect to see. Over a few years, an atmosphere of discontent built up among the farmers that "their" harvest festival was being taken over, and it has taken hard work by the Provost and a carefully-chosen committee to readjust the balance and to make the festival a valued part of the farming year. Even then, placing a combine harvester on Cathedral Green, to complement an exhibition of children's work and a variety of livestock, drew the comment from one local farmer: "I know what a bloody combine looks like!" (Having almost lost half the choirboys into the cutter bar, the combine might be dispensed with next year.)

There is still a divide in many villages between the farmers and the farm workers – a divide that will not be bridged by special services, as they probably would not come together. And yet the cleric is probably the only person who has regular contact with both; he or she is still welcome in the houses of both, and sometimes has to intercede between the two. A lot of pastoral work is done by the wave as you wait for their tractors to go past, and your willingness to talk to them when you go to the farm to see the boss.

Old villagers, those who have lived there for many years, can be the hardest to get to know and to make contact with. A few will be churchgoers and will be easier to meet, but many will have seen so many rectors – each one, supposedly, worse than the one before – and anything you can do will simply be irrelevant to them, until someone dies. For the older villagers, the church still comes into its own for a funeral; even if they never even darken the door at Christmas, the funeral and burial will still take place in the village. It needs to be traditional enough to please, and if you have to do the homily you have to have your facts right; so it will take a long time to write as you must visit several folk to find out what you should know. The "bunfight" afterwards will be even more important than the service, but there comes a time when the cleric should leave to let the serious drinking start. Pastoral work after the event should include a visit to the over-60s as soon as possible.

Newer villagers may well not have their funeral in the village church; they will go straight to the crematorium. We are fortunate in Suffolk that the funeral directors always contact their village cleric to take the service, so a pastoral link can be built up. The downside is the length of time it takes to go to a crematorium as opposed to the church, and I find it hard coping with the fact that they don't want to use their village church. It seems to me to be a worrying trend that fewer and fewer occasional offices take place in the village church, which means it has less and less of a place in people's understanding of what makes a village.

I thought this would happen with weddings, as more and more secular venues open up, but it seems to have made little impact on the number of marriages in my churches. I don't know if anyone has done any research on the subject, but I wonder if it is mainly urban couples now using these pretty venues, rather than village couples who already have them? What worries me is that the marriage legislation, if properly applied, makes it impossible for many to get married in our village churches. Residence qualifications were no bar when the daughter lived in the family home until her wedding, but these days the daughter is usually living with her partner in the nearest town. However, the village church is still "home", and that is where they want to marry. If I say "No", then I upset the bride and her parents, so most of us define residence very, very widely. But surely there is an urgent need for a rewrite of the legislation. There are so many venues – all marketing themselves so hard – and yet the Church puts up barriers which stop people marrying where they want to.

From a practical point of view, I need as many weddings as possible; we need the fees and we need the goodwill. From a theological point of view, if I believe a successful life needs founding on God, let alone a successful marriage, then I want people to start their marriage with worship, prayer and God's blessing. There will be some couples who try to twist me round their little fingers and whom I never see again, but most of them will appreciate their wedding, and appreciate a Christmas card, and will come to midnight mass when they come home. They will probably have had to visit their own parish priest for the calling of the banns – even if the bride-to-be has given her residence as being in my village, her partner will probably be resident where they are living. And if they are welcomed there, a relationship with the church can start. Even if that relationship does not develop, marriage is a sacrament, and sacraments depend firstly on God's grace.

A number of wedding couples will turn up a few years later for a baptism, and again it is good to say "Yes". I always insist that they go to see their home parish priest for him/her to sign a consent form, creating an opportunity for a relationship to start there, and I am one of those difficult clergy who insist on a baptism taking place during the main Sunday service. Some colleagues disagree on this, arguing that refusal to baptise at 3pm on a Sunday can do as much damage as refusing to marry. I argue that the benefits of having the whole family at an enjoyable family service outweigh the disadvantage. I am not keen on christening at a Eucharist; unless the family are churchgoers, I do not think that is a helpful introduction, and the regular congregation seems to accept their family service being a somewhat movable feast to fit the families. (As long as they have their 8am Book of Common Prayer communion, most will be happy – "community" only goes so far!) Families do seem to delay baptism more and more – "cost" is usually given as the reason – but a regular visit to Mums and Toddlers helps to keep the presence of the church alive.

We have found it useful to hold regular children's workshops throughout the year, on a Saturday afternoon before a family service, and these have been excellent ways of making contacts with children and parents. Having a church school is a wonderful way into that age range, although school boundaries so rarely fit benefice boundaries that it can be a problem to connect with all. In Suffolk, children leave their village school when they are nine to go to middle schools, and that makes long-term relationships with the church difficult. In one village, a summer pantomime was superb at keeping me in touch with the teenagers – I'm a wonderful Friar Tuck – but now I'm persona non grata in the other large village because I was not in their summer production.

That perhaps sums up the church's role in the community – the tension as we try to involve ourselves. If we build up people's expectations that we will be involved, the day comes when we cannot be in six places at once. Usually people will understand, but sometimes they will not. Most parishioners have smaller orbits than the cleric – they will concentrate on their village, while we will have several to deal with – and they do not always understand when their orbit is not as important to you as it is to them. Tensions between communities often exist and, as the only person trying to cover both, the cleric can get hurt. For example, it seemed a good idea to put a page about the school in the magazine that covers the four villages, as a way of letting the community know what was going on. But the village whose catchment school is different are furious that the first is "advertising itself". Questions have been asked at the parish council, and it's the rector's fault.

Sometimes you become the Aunt Sally because many people want a church that is not too close, and a rector who wears a sweatshirt and who goes to village functions is dangerously normal. Within recent memory, the rector lived in one of the largest houses; you stood and tugged your forelock when he walked in to school. It is "not right" when he lives in a reasonable modern house, drives into your village, and then drives out again. Rural people have long memories, and many have convinced themselves that they were happier with that sort of hierarchy and relationship.

But the dog collar still has power that perhaps has gone from other aspects of life. One colleague commented that public school taught "how to run the country, and to be nice to the clergy". It gets me through the majority of doors in the village. People are not surprised when I turn up in hospital to see them – as long as someone else has told me that they're in – and no one thinks I should be "police checked" before I visit playgroup. This, to me, is the privilege of being in a rural community, and one the Church must repay by being there for all.

That is easier said than done. I cannot physically be in every church every Sunday, and it would make much more sense if the congregations all came to one place. Sometimes we are right to insist on it; they need to know that the Christian church is bigger than their single-figures. But on most occasions we must be where the people want us to be. Yet it can be so very depressing always having "lovely little services", always dealing with the small numbers. Then a new family, just moved into the village from a lively suburban church, announce that they will be driving to town every Sunday, and you wonder why you bother. There are times when it seems that my only use is to draw the obligatory raffle at any fund-raising event, and that it is only the church building that matters.

Finally, there is the all-important question of the building and finance – around which much of my life seems to revolve.

One church has just raised £35,000 and is waiting for work to start (when English Heritage sort themselves out); another needs £100,000 and has reached £80,000; the third needs £30,000 and can't bring itself to start fund-raising (indeed, we are having to look seriously at closure); the fourth had the quinquennial report done before I arrived, and I have not dared read it. Three pay their quota, one can not – and the other three will not help it. Much of our life, as the regular congregations, revolves around these practicalities, and if anything will sink them it will be this. But the huge quota increases of the past have largely been coped with, the 17.5 per cent VAT on repairs will somehow be found (surely its abolition would be a huge rural vote winner?), and we will still be here and still open long after the present rector has gone.

One of my churches was standing at time of the last Millennium. It has seen more changes in community than anyone would have thought possible – and it has survived.

The **Rev. Peter Barham** is priest-in-charge of Bradfield St Clare, Cockfield, Felsham and Gedding, near Bury St Edmunds.

Chapter Nine

Learning curve:
The Church and schools

by Richard Lindley

Starting socially valuable projects and movements, then gradually handing them over to the State, has been the Church's pioneering role in Britain and across the world. To a large degree, this applies to education as much as to medical and social care. What is unique about education in England and Wales is that the Church has retained its institutional stake – particularly in the provision of schools – even though the State meets the lion's share of the costs. Many of the independent schools were founded on a church-affiliated basis, even though owned by private trusts, organisations and individuals. But in the majority state-funded sector of what are termed "maintained" schools, almost one third are church schools (21.7 per cent Church of England, 9.7 per cent Roman Catholic and around 1 per cent Methodist and other Christian, with the small group of ecumenical Catholic-Anglican and Methodist-Anglican schools probably also within the 1 per cent). There are also a handful of "maintained" Jewish schools, and, recently, just two "maintained" Muslim schools.

Until the latter part of the 19th century, all schools were church schools – many with origins lost in the mists of time, and often originally run by the clergy in their churches. The 19th century saw a vast programme of school building by the churches, and in 1833 state money was made available for the first time to support them. Local Education Authorities did not appear until 1902, but "county" schools (as schools provided by LEAs later came to be called, and now restyled "community" schools) find their origin in the "Board" schools set up after 1870 to plug the gaps left by the churches. The system became known as the "dual" system, with the Church firmly entrenched in the legal framework – particularly the 1944 Education Act, and all subsequent legislation through to the School Standards and Framework Act of 1998. Alongside a renewed place for

LEAs (particularly for improving standards in schools) after 10 years in a comparative wilderness, the 1998 Act seems to place more emphasis on the distinctiveness of church schools, and gives diocesan authorities more responsibilities than ever before.

An indicator of government perception of the role of the Church is the legislation concerning church representation on LEA education committees. The 1944 Act recommended voting membership for church representatives alongside other community representatives, and this was reinforced in 1972. From 1989 (further clarified in 1994), it became mandatory for the Church of England/Church in Wales (henceforward referred to as the Anglican Church) and the Roman Catholic Church to have voting membership, but this was on grounds of their provision of schools. The implication was that the purpose was to enable the churches to defend their corner, rather than to share concern and responsibility for all schools as they had previously seen themselves as doing.

With few exceptions, however, the two Churches' representatives have continued to express themselves – and, hopefully, a Christian perspective – on topics of all kinds relating to any or all schools, while of course looking to the particular interests of church schools and religious education. The risk is of de-skilling or de-mobilising Christian councillors, who might otherwise allow their faith to influence their conduct. The hope is that, in the party politicised local authority context, the Church's representatives might encourage them by their presence and utterances.

The 1998 legislation brings diocesan representation not only on LEA education committees and sub-committees, but also on the new Schools Organisation Committee and Admissions Forum(s) for each LEA. Although the government's intention is again to give the churches an opportunity to defend their corner, the churches will undoubtedly see the opportuntity as a responsibility to share in decision-making for the good of all the schools in an LEA area.

There are two further LEA bodies, of a less political nature, where all the main churches have had membership, often since 1944. These are the Standing Advisory Council on Religious Education (SACRE) and the associated Agreed Syllabus Conference. An "agreed syllabus" is the RE syllabus for the "community" schools and some categories of church schools. It is "agreed" in that four groups must agree to recommend the finished product to the education committee for adoption – the four groups representing the LEA itself, the Church of England (in England), other religious groups (from Muslims to Methodists, and including the Catholic Church and, in Wales, the Church in Wales) and teacher organisations. The SACRE operates on a similar basis, but advises the education committee and its officers on matters relating to RE and collective worship.

All pupils (unless withdrawn by their parents) at all "community" and some church schools must be taught RE, with a predominance of Christianity but with material about other major religions. Similarly, all pupils must attend daily collective worship – either for the whole school or in class or other tutor groups – that is "wholly or mainly or a broadly Christian character". If a school feels in all conscience that it cannot deliver because of the religious tradition of its pupils, then the SACRE can grant a dispensation from the "Christian" requirement, though daily collective worship of some sort must remain. At all church schools, collective worship can follow the pattern of the providing church, and in certain categories of church schools RE too can be denominational.

Immediately, church schools find themselves with questions about their mission – in both the secular and religious meanings of "mission". Like the best of corporate institutions nowadays, all schools are expected to have mission statements, and some are very explicit about the school's Christian aims – for example, "to live and grow together as friends and disciples of Christ". Under the terms of the 1998 Act, all church schools have also been required to publish "ethos statements", which are often similar in content. Church schools therefore need to be explicit about their mission in the secular sense: whether their mission will include mission in the Christian sense; and, if it does, what the nature of that Christian mission will be.

Put another way, a church school has to decide whether it sees itself, and wishes others to view it, as an extension of the parochial church community, an embodiment of Christian community; or, alternatively, whether it aspires to be an activity of the church community outwards into the separate, local, secular community. Put yet another way, in terms of the admission of children, a church school has to decide whether priority will be given to the children of church-going families, or else to neighbourhood families irrespective of their beliefs or religious practices.

The position of Roman Catholic schools is traditionally the clearer. Catholic schools were provided for Catholic children, with an expectation that every Catholic child would attend one in preference to any other school. Thus there is virtually universal coverage, with both primary schools and secondary schools placed to meet the needs of most families. Catholic faith – on the part of teachers and children alike – is assumed, and the life of the school echoes and exemplifies Catholic faith and practice. However, demand from Catholic families has fallen in many areas. Conversely, demand for places at Catholic schools has risen from non-Catholic families who are nominally or actively members of other Christian churches and – most confusingly of all – from Muslims, Hindus and Sikhs in urban areas. Government "open enrolment" policy and the need to sustain a school budget (now based largely on pupil numbers) have presented the Catholic Church both with a dilemma and a challenge, and have required fresh thinking about the mission of its schools, in both senses of the word.

For Anglican schools, the position has been less painful, but there is still a new challenge that has emerged. These schools were not established primarily to do a denominational job. Although church teaching and worship were prescribed, most of these schools were provided principally as neighbourhood schools for children who were otherwise receiving no education at all. Nineteenth-century trust deeds often refer to "children of the poor and labouring classes of the parish". This tradition has continued, both in small towns and villages where the church school was the only local option, and also to a large extent in urban areas, even though there would be other options open to those preferring a non-church school.

The tradition has been encouraged since 1944 by the existence of two main kinds of Anglican schools, with around half as many again being of the "voluntary controlled" variety, rather than "voluntary aided". (All Catholic schools are "aided".) The words "controlled" and "aided" refer to the extent of LEA influence that pervaded until 1988, with the diocese and parish church having considerably more opportunity for influence in aided schools. Although controlled schools are very much church schools, the Church has, with some exceptions, underplayed its hand, believing in some way that they have not been "real" church schools because the Church has not appointed a majority of governors and because most RE has followed the local "agreed" syllabus. Inevitably, "aided" schools in some parishes have to some extent been undervalued along with them.

But now all of that is changing for Anglican schools. The denominational inspection system that accompanies the OFSTED inspection regime has meant that all church schools are inspected every few years, with a report being published and then an action plan as to what the school intends to do about deficiencies that have been observed. So far, the rigour of these inspections has been less than that exercised by OFSTED. Although dioceses advise over the appointment of the denominational inspector from an approved list, it is not helpful that – unlike with the main OFSTED inspection – the school governors, in the final analysis, appoint their own inspector. The yardsticks employed by some inspectors reflect the relatively low expectations that prevail in some Anglican quarters. The Church may well be failing parents in this respect. Having chosen church schools for their children, the overall impression is that the majority are prepared for far more by way of Christian teaching and sacramental life than most church schools offer.

With honourable exceptions, the bulk of Anglican schools have been failing the Church in this respect. But the tide may be turning, as the Church realises the huge asset that exists in its schools. There are probably more people living in Christian community and worshipping together five days a week in Church of England/Church in Wales schools than gather in her churches Sunday by Sunday. Under the influence of the Decade of Evangelism, the inspection regime and a general renewal of confidence – and supported by enhanced provisions in the 1998 Education Act – churches and their schools are growing together. School Eucharists are becoming more common, held both in church and in school. Confirmation preparation will follow – the period of preparation perhaps straddling children's entry into secondary school, so that individual commitment and decision are preserved. Then family involvement will come too.

For both Catholic as well as Church of England/Church in Wales schools, nothing of this in any way need subvert the neighbourhood function of schools. Of course, the mission (both secular and Christian) of an urban school with a 98 per cent

Muslim population will differ from what has been described. Of course, school Eucharists will be inappropriate there. However, the challenge there is work out a new Christian vocation, rather than to brush Christian identity under the carpet. The challenge will consist of a dialogue of faith with the mosque that results in mutual experiences of religious practice and a shared understanding of the Church's role in enabling children's spiritual development to take place on that basis.

Some years ago, some bold preparations were made for Muslims to share in the governance of an inner-city church secondary school that was to provide for the legitimate cultural and spiritual development of Asian girls – some of whom were then not currently attending school at all. Some exhilarating inter-faith dialogue occurred, as plans were hammered out for "modesty" washing facilities, swimming arrangements and the like, and as interesting debate about Islamic attitudes to music and dance resulted in workable compromise about curriculum content. Neither the existing governors, nor the diocese, not the mosque withdrew from the planning process. But the scheme was scuppered by the then Secretary of State when formal proposals were published and refused.

Of course, most church schools do not have 98 per cent Muslims attending. Even so, there will be others where Christian vocation and service take a form different from the close relationship with church life that has been described. However, many church schools are very attractive to families of faiths other than Christianity. Church schools are valued as places of clear morality, God-centred, and with a clear presentation of the Christian faith and practices. The clearer the Christian identity, sometimes it seems the more demand there is from Hindus, Muslims and Sikhs. For with clear Christian values often comes a clear recognition of the multi-cultural openness of Christ himself, allowing space for faith development for all.

These matters are of particular and immediate concern for church schools in urban areas with multi-ethnic populations. Church schools should be in the vanguard of multi-cultural concern – and the indications are that they usually are. This is not to imply any "watering down" of Christian vocation, identity or mission. What it does imply is a directing of those qualities into channels that bespeak selfless service, opportunity for "spiritual, moral, social and cultural" development on the part of all pupils, and open dialogue and growth of mutual understanding between people of all the great faiths. Alongside this openness of spirit, however, people of other faiths expect to see a joyful maximisation of the Christian opportunities that church schools offer the Christian community.

Pretending not to be a church school at all – in terms of actual activity, if not in words – is just confusing for all concerned, and a travesty of the confidence of those who made sacrifices to found and maintain the school. Dialogue from a position of evident confidence is more impressive. Dialogue that then wants to meet the reasonable religious and cultural needs of peoples of other faiths is more impressive still. The establishment of two Muslim schools in the "maintained" sector should do wonders to reassure the wider Muslim communities of London and Birmingham of the nation's regard for their faith. It may ease the tension in those areas over religious education and collective worship generally, even though only a minority of Muslim children will attend just two small schools. The Church, and its schools close by, should be supporting them.

The challenges for church schools in areas without significant Asian and Black populations are at least as great. Racism is often latent – not malicious or deliberate, but based on ignorance, nervousness and lack of direct contact with people of other racial backgrounds and religions. It shows itself unexpectedly, in the unguarded moments of sudden encounter. Fear of the unknown can lead to narrowness of vision, justified in religious terms by the "uniqueness" claims of the Bible being taken out of the context of the life of Jesus himself, who dealt gently with people of a variety of cultures and religions and tended to forecast judgment on the basis of human kindness rather than doctrines held dear. A strong Christian identity will foster multi-cultural generosity without any detriment to the church nature of a church school.

So the norm will remain the school that is one with its parish church – part and parcel of each other, complementary as two centres of Christian life, education and worship in their parish. Within the Anglican Church at least, the issue is one of raising expectations, with the onus resting first on the bishops, synods, diocesan boards of education, diocesan education officers, local churches and, above all, parish clergy. With expectations raised in those quarters, the legal framework is in place for church schools to take off with their distinctive nature in a way they never have before. There is nevertheless room for improvement in the denominational inspection routine, with a more stringent framework and more rigorous training of inspectors – and the weeding out of some.

Church schools are somewhat caught between two cultures. The educational world is now one of accountability, monitoring and feedback. Time and energy are fully occupied in fulfilling the demands of the budget sheet, development plans, action plans and test results. But the ecclesiastical world is characterised by almost no accountability (at least in worldly terms!), monitoring or feedback. So the danger is that the distinctive nature of a church school may be neglected unless the inspection is as thorough as the OFSTED one, and the yardstick sufficiently demanding in recovering the explicit Christian nature of the school. Perhaps we need a daily RE and Worship Hour to complement the new Literacy and Numeracy Hours, and "Ecclesiastical Special Measures" to complement the naming-and-shaming Special Measures to which schools are consigned for a while if they fail their OFSTED inspections.

So there is much room for improvement, whether church schools serve the families of leafy suburbs, decayed urban areas or supposed rural idylls. But the fact remains that, in the educational sector, the Church has an institutional stake as a provider unlike any other role, apart from that of Westminster Abbey as a purveyor of Coronations and Royal Weddings. The present government has shown itself more concerned to support this participation that has been the case for many a year. But the test is whether the Church will rise to the challenge and to the opportunity. It may not come again.

Richard Lindley is director of education for the Winchester Diocese and was formerly director of education for the Birmingham Diocese.

Chapter Ten

Healing words: Health and the Church

by Terry Drummond

The issue of health in the context of the local church is one that is often linked inextricably in the mind of the average church member to the question of healing. Many churches hold regular healing services, and prayers for the sick are rightly included as a part of the periods of intercession in most of acts of worship. In some traditions there is also a history of regular pilgrimages to holy shrines such as Lourdes, particularly for those with physical ailments, who may be seeking consolation and affirmation or even the possibility of miraculous cure.

In linking the work and ministry of the Christian disciple with these particular responses to illness, there is a danger that any discussion of health care both for the ordained and lay person is lost in the more specific discussion of medicine and medical care. This is underlined by the work of those theologians who work in the specific areas of exploring the limits to medical care and in genetic engineering. These can become the subject of wide-ranging public debate and can overwhelm the potential for a wider discussion on the more fundamental issue of what is actually understood by health.

In addition, the Bible can at times manage to obscure the issue due to the emphasis on stories of healing – from the story of Naaman the Syrian, who suffered from leprosy (2 Kings, chapter 5), through to the New Testament healing miracles of Jesus and to those recorded in the Acts of the Apostles. These become the bench marks for some Christians who seek a return to the times of miraculous healing, to the detriment of the wider understanding of health as a key element of wholeness.

The over-emphasis on healing in the context of the ministry of Jesus is to miss his challenge to those He met that they should become whole people – as seen in the story of the representative of the ruling class who sought teaching on eternal life (Luke 18) and in the teaching of the beatitudes (Matthew 5), both of which point to a more rounded understanding of what it is to be fully human.

The possibility of wholeness in the biblical tradition is pointed out in the Jubilee Centre publication *Biblical Perspectives on Health and Health Care Relationships*, and specifically in discussing the word "shalom". The authors note that "most contemporary theologians agree that 'shalom ' is the nearest Hebrew dynamic equivalent to the word 'health'." This is followed by a quotation from an essay by David Atkinson, in which he writes: "Health is clearly part of shalom, as can be illustrated by the numerous times in the Old Testament when shalom is bracketed together with a Hebrew word translated as 'health' or 'healing'. Thus the vision of peace in Isaiah 2: 1-5 (which could almost stand as a definition of shalom) is set in contrast to the sickness of the nation (1: 5-6), its idolatry (2: 6-22) and social injustice (3: 13-15) which brings the judgment that the Lord will not be a healer (3: 7b)."

In opening a discussion on the place of health in the Christian life, by trying to define a starting point different from those associated with healing, it is important to reiterate the point that healing is not to be ignored, but that the discussion should be shifted to a different focus. In this context, it is important to define what is actually meant by the word health.

The World Health Organisation (WHO) stated in 1948 that "health is a state of complete physical, mental and social well being and not merely the absence of disease or infirmity". The Labour government elected in 1997 opened its green paper on health, *Our Healthier Nation*: "Good health. It's not just a toast. It's what everybody wants for themselves, their family and friends. If you are a parent, it's the supreme gift you'd like to give your children. For the sake of every individual, for society and for the economy, it should be a top priority for any government. It is a top priority for this government."

The exploration of a Christian approach to these issues can use both these quotations as a starting point for recovering an understanding of what we mean by health. The WHO definition is quite restrictive, in so far as its starting point remains a medical approach and maintains the link between ill health and wholeness of life. The Labour government's statement, on the other hand, is a positive affirmation of the benefits associated with good health, which can be a cause for celebration.

The linkage of health to the Christian faith is not only a response to a theological approach and understanding, it can also draw on the long Christian history of the practical responses of service – encapsulated in the way that the Church, through the monastic tradition, opened some of the earliest hospitals. The foundation of many modern hospitals came from this source.

To move the discussion forward, it is important to see the whole area being under review, and in particular to move way from the restrictions inherent in a medical model of health care. The shift of emphasis will be into an understanding of what is described in the term social/public health; it is a move that takes in issues relating to environment, such as air and water quality, housing and issues relating to transport. The effects of poor quality services in these areas can be detrimental to people wherever they live, but especially for those in urban communities where, due to the density of population, the potential for such problems are more obvious.

The move into the wider context of a discussion of health care and provision will, for some Christians, be a new experience. For others, the liberation that will come with a changed understanding of the work they are doing will offer opportunities to consider potential new avenues and ways of thinking about existing projects and their development. Consideration of the Church's work in this area will include discussion across a wide range of issues that relate to understanding and promoting what is meant by better health.

It is important to identify the themes that will underpin a Christian approach. These include:

• Individuals' personal responsibility for their own health;

• Links into the wider community, and a shared responsibility for the neighbourhoods that the Church seeks to serve;

• Contributing to local policy-making on the most effective health care, both in a local area and in the wider community/borough.

All of these issues are interrelated and juxtapose both a concern for the individual and the development of personal discipleship, while not losing sight of the contribution that is rooted in the local neighbourhood and is also concerned with the wider community.

In considering how individuals make a personal response to the issues, the question becomes one of how Christians seek to live out a healthy lifestyle – that is, one based on a holistic approach to living, bringing together an understanding of the spiritual and physical nature of life.

The starting point for this approach to developing a healthier lifestyle can be by making use of health education. It is of particular importance to understand how to respond to issues such as smoking and its effect both on the individual and those they come into contact with. The organisation of smoking cessation classes for church members may be a starting point, with the issue being addressed through talks to church groups. Equally, there could be a policy on alcohol consumption that recognises the particular needs of those who have a problem with over-consumption. It is not necessary to stop all alcohol at functions or parties, but it is important to recognise the need for adult non-alcoholic drinks to be available; a glass of sickly orange juice, bought for the children, is not an alternative.

The issues associated with smoking and drinking are the easiest to respond to when it comes to a local church trying to work out what it can do to promote better health. They are the easiest because they are the subjects of a great deal of public debate within the wider community. They represent the most obvious socially-available drugs within the community, and the use of one and the over-consumption of the other are major causes of ill health. The fact that they are in such popular use should not detract from understanding their potential ill effects.

The misuse of illegal drugs, and a greater understanding of their effects both on residents and local communities, is a further important stage in consideration of the Church's role in working for better health. It is probable that most drug abusers will not attend church, though it should no be ruled out as a possibility, and in some families within the church community there may well be drug users within the family network. The role of the Church and its worshipping members may be to offer support to those working in the field of drug abuse, and equally being informed on the effects that misuse can have. Many local authorities produce information packs, and their distribution through church networks will assist in taking the debate on drugs into a wider area. This is especially true when a church is linked in to local schools.

The problems in this field have been most clearly identified within urban communities, and in particular the inner urban areas and outer estates, but the most recent research also points to wide-ranging heroin abuse in rural areas. Wherever the issues arise there is a task for church people, both laity and clergy, to be informed and involved in seeking to work out positive responses to the problems that can develop in local areas.

It is important that, having identified specific areas for potential action by the local church, there is also a better understanding of what is actually meant by health. And, in moving away from the specific issue of healing, a definition that is theologically valid must be used in the debate about the contribution of the Church both to the delivery of practical services and education.

The issues outlined above should not detract from the wider implications of seeking a healthy lifestyle and a holistic approach to life. The local church can, in addition, use its teaching programme to put forward ideas and to encourage congregations to think about health, both in the context of spirituality and personal well being. A challenge is to avoid the potential of being seen as killjoys, when the opposite is actually the truth. The GP/priest Michael Wilson puts the argument for health in the Christian life as follows: "Healthy for what? For God. For that which is at the heart of all that is, in which we live and move and have our being. For the ultimate context. The experience of health, because it is the foretaste of wholeness to come, contains the beauty, love and joy, the answer in itself. For what are we healthy? Just for the fun of it!"

If we are to take these words seriously, there will also need to be a shift away from the needs of individuals, into thinking about the wider community and into a celebration of wholeness that is possible when groups recognise new ways of sharing. The move into thinking in this wider sense brings demands for new forms of pastoral ministry that will promote action on behalf of all who live in a local community. Any church extending its thinking into what might be a new and wider area of work will need to identify and establish a strategy for its actions. These could include:

• Promoting understanding within the Christian community/congregation;

- Taking the message into the wider community'

- Identifying, and responding to, local parish neighbourhood needs.

Promoting the issues in the church community and congregation will be to build on all of the above, making use of teaching sessions such as the Sunday sermon and midweek groups. The role of regular meetings, such as an elderly persons' luncheon club, should not be underestimated. Regular gatherings of people for other activities can and should be used to broaden the spreading of information.

The linking into the wider community can be a part of a strategy that encourages the congregation to be involved in the life of the neighbourhood. It is of particular importance that in areas of social deprivation the health of the community is recognised as being a key element in understanding the area. Problems associated with poor diet, low income and regular periods of ill health for local residents can be a focus for the Church to enter into a partnership with the health authority to promote a better understanding of local health needs. In addition, alliances with local groups can be used to argue for an improvement in services.

An underestimated resource in this context is the Church's buildings; in some areas, they are the only public communal space. Opening up these buildings for wider use can be a major step in allowing people to come together for a wider discussion of the issues that effect their lives. The church community with a vision for its area may want to be involved in local social or health needs assessment. These are reviews of an area's health and social needs, undertaken by professionals but always in partnership with local people.

The assessment allows for a full review of local social need – be it an improvement in the availability of doctors' surgeries or the need for more green space. A survey undertaken in the parish of All Saints, Hackbridge, in the London borough of Sutton, as part of a wider assessment in an area with Single Regeneration Funding, included three church members, the church's community development officer and had the backing of the vicar and the PCC.

The results included a critical response to health issue in the area, the summary being:

- More health information and education – for children, and also on specific issues such as menopause and breast feeding.

- Need for interpersonal skills of GPs' receptionists to be addressed and for shorter waiting times.

- Concern about funding and efficiency in hospital in general, and about accident and emergency care in particular.

- Concern about funding and efficiency in health authority.

- Lack of care for elderly and support for carers.

- Importance of antenatal and postnatal care.

An important element of this survey was the use of local people in the interviewing and the large cross-section of the community that expressed opinions, from children through to the elderly. A part of the report offers an older women's perceptions of health: "We asked them to think of any ideas they associated with 'health'. Initially, they mentioned food, fitness and physical wellbeing, but went on to include ideas about stress – and related factors, such as safety, noise, travel, friendliness and religion."

The importance of this kind of assessment lies in the fact that it can include a review of all the issues – including health – that affect local communities, and part of its importance is that it informs local policy makers and provides evidence for local people who are seeking to improve services. The Church's role is to encourage participation by its own worshipping community, as well as the local residents, and to offer – where it is appropriate – space for people to meet. A particular contribution may be to host the meeting when the information is disseminated. The report can, in addition, be used by the parochial church council to underpin its strategy for local mission and outreach.

The contribution made by the Church can be seen to bring added value to the debate, through offering support and resources to those who are seeking to improve local health care and by being open to the community. The potential for developing this area of work is of particular importance in contributing to the debate on the question of health variations (previously known as health inequalities) which underpins the development both of local and national policy. In this context, churches which are in areas of deprivation may also be in Health Action Zones (HAZs), areas set aside by government for extra investment in health and social services and which will seek to combat both health inequalities and poverty.

The document published by the Department of Health outlining the purpose and aims of HAZs, and inviting bids from the relevant authorities, stated that the HAZ would include in its aims identifying and addressing the public health needs of the local area through: "empowering people and giving them the tools to take greater responsibility for their own health; building on existing strengths in the local community to achieve a sustainable capability; and focusing on those whose needs are greatest and implementing plans to reduce health inequalities.".

A specific emphasis of the HAZ is that all of the work is to be a partnership between both the statutory authorities and local community groups and others with an interest in combating inequalities in whatever form they are manifested. This gives an active local church a natural entry point to contribute to their development and to work in partnership with other groups.

The third area for consideration is to ensure that any work on improving health is based on a relevant response to local needs. In so doing, the emphasis must be shifted from the traditional approach of medical care to recognising that social/public health leads to a broader understanding of the links between health and a wide range of issues. These include the outcomes associated with local environmental problems; for example, areas with high levels of traffic pollution are often those with high levels of asthma in young children. In addition, poor housing contributes to poor health, and low income is often linked to poor diet, which can lead to ill health in both the young and the old.

The role of the Church in responding to these needs will include assisting in setting up action groups to combat the particular problems – in the case of poor air quality, for example, by gathering evidence that can be used to argue for a change in local transport/roads policy. The issue of poor housing may lead to tenants' groups which can challenge the landlord with evidence based not only on the state of the housing, but also on information about the state of the residents' health. The question of diet can be raised through the work described above, by working with existing groups who meet together, or by serious thought being given to setting up food co-ops and communal gardens for growing fresh food. All of these responses can have a long-term effect on the health and life of a local community, contributing to the sustainability of the area and any new projects that develop out of the consultations.

In becoming involved in these issues and problems, the Church is able to extend its mission and assist in moving the debate on health out of the sterilised corridors of health authorities and other public bodies and into the centre of communities. It can ensure that the discussion is taken up by those who are most effected – the ordinary citizens who often do not know how to access those with authority. The setting up of HAZs will no doubt lead to these issues being promoted and developed within the designated areas, but it is important that those communities with no special government action plan or programmes are also facing up to the challenge.

The potential for the renewal of areas and the provision of better facilities for local people are the main aims of these new programmes, be they Health or Education Action Zones. For the local Christian community, the challenge is to ensure that specific initiatives that improve the quality of life are a continuing aim within an overall strategy for mission.

All of the above is based on a premise that, to develop new work, the local church will be prepared to seek new partners in the programmes they develop. In the case of health, contact with the local health authority is the most obvious example, though links with local authority departments will also be necessary. Local regeneration initiatives have, in the past, tended not to see health as a part of their work. In the future, this is less likely to be the case. The government, in its plan to combat social exclusion, sees these policies as being interrelated.

The local church that is active within its local community can build on existing partnerships with other Christian organisations, the wider voluntary sector and, on occasion, the business community. The development in the coming years of new projects – particularly those, such as Healthy Living Centres, whose aim is to serve the whole community – will only be supported by the government when there are partnerships in existence.

The churches must recognise the potential that working with partners – be they other churches or local groups – will put them in a stronger position to offer a better service to those who live in the area they serve, bringing together a concern for spiritual health and wellbeing with that of the physical health of people. The partnership will also lead to conversations on why the Church is concerned with issues that have traditionally been the preserve of specialists. Promoting better health can open up the possibilities of speaking of the wholeness for all human beings that is central to the Christian message.

The partnerships, as pointed out above, can lead to the fuller use of church buildings and premises. Many examples exist of churches offering care to the homeless – for example, St Botolphs, Aldgate, in the City of London, and St Petrock's in Exeter. Others have opened up health facilities to serve the wider community; the Bromley by Bow Centre in East London, with its GP facilities, is the best example of this way of working. These three projects are large in scale, with budgets to match, but the small local church should not be put off by this fact.

The organisation Community Health UK has been working on an action research project on Promoting Health in Places of Worship, and this multi-faith initiative has produced some interesting examples of what is possible. In a list of projects and activities published in the report of a consultation on the issue, the following are listed as examples:

- A community cafe.

- Parent and toddler groups.

- Health clinics.

- Healthy eating.

- Alcoholics Anonymous.

- Look after your heart.

But these are only a small cross-section of the kind of work that is possible, and that can be promoted within church premises. Any group considering developing work in this context may well find it beneficial to learn from others who have already shown a way forward.

The promotion and better understanding of what is meant

by health is a key concern of many policy-makers, and it is important to reiterate the need for the Church at large to be open to new ideas and developments. The move away from a medical understanding of physical health into a wider holistic approach opens up infinite possibilities for action that will proclaim an understanding of God's care for the whole of humanity and reinforce the Church's mission to the whole community. The development of partnerships with other bodies, and a commitment to outreach, will assist in the improvement of health for the poor and send a clear message to the wider community.

Terry Drummond is adviser on social responsibility and industrial mission for the Croydon episcopal area and is Chair of Community Health UK.

Selected reading

Biblical Perspectives on Health Care and Health Care Relationships (Jubilee Centre, Cambridge. 1998).

Christian Healing: What Can We Believe? (Lynx Communications. SPCK, London. 1997).

Our Healthier Nation (Stationery Office, London. 1998).

Health is For People, by Michael Wilson (Darton Longman and Todd, London. 1975).

Health Action Zones. Invitation to Bid (NHS Executive, Leeds. 1998).

Drummond, Hole and Chapman *Promoting Health Through Places of Worship* (Community Health UK, 4 – 5 Bridge Street, Bath BA2 4AS).

Chapter Eleven

Finding a voice: Women's perspective

by Denise Mumford

A little over a century ago, the novelist Charlotte M. Yonge confirmed that women believed in themselves as lesser mortals. "I have no hesitation in declaring," she wrote in 1889, "my full belief in the inferiority of woman, nor that she has brought it upon herself. It was the woman who was the first to fall and to draw her husband into the same transgression. Thence her punishment of physical weakness and subordination." In any consideration of women in relation to the church as community, or the church in community, such attitudes must be taken into account. What women have achieved has been – and still is, to some degree – moulded by the perceptions of their capabilities.

During the 20th century some extraordinary changes have taken place in women's lives. In education, compulsory schooling for girls up to the age of 16 was introduced; women were finally admitted to the universities, and now have equality (or better) with boys and men in educational achievement at all levels. In political life, women were given the vote; the first woman took her seat in Parliament in 1919, and by 1979 Britain had its first woman Prime Minister. Women are now able to control the size of their families through contraception, and to apply for custody of their children in the courts in the event of separation from a spouse. Divorce is no longer difficult to achieve, and many women have at least a period in their lives when they are single parents. People are living longer, and most elderly people are women. At work, Equal Pay and Sex Discrimination Acts have started to create better opportunities for women in the workplace. There are many more women at work: the 1991 Census showed that 47 per cent of the workforce were women, and the number is growing.

The combination of this rapid social change and the deep-seated, derogatory attitudes towards women has left men and women confused about their roles in relation to each other.

Many injustices to women remain, and men, who still hold the balance of power in society, attempt to maintain the status quo. The age-old message that caring, for all generations, is the job of the woman at the centre of the family has not changed. Guilt, as well as love, is the spur. Moreover, although some social changes have greatly improved women's lives, new problems have arisen out of them, causing confusion and stress. An example is how to combine child rearing and work.

The Church has been one of the most conservative institutions in its response to women and their contribution to society. Women felt for many generations that it would be wrong to break out of their traditional roles. Theology has been used relentlessly to reinforce patriarchal attitudes. The issue of "headship", still debated hotly, arises in a number of biblical texts, for example in Ephesians 5:22: "Women be subject to your husbands, as to the Lord; for the man is head of the woman, just as Christ is head of the church . . ." And this is by no means a dead issue: in June 1998, the Southern Baptists – America's largest Protestant group, with 16 million members – amended their statement of beliefs to include the declaration that a wife must "submit herself graciously" to her husband's leadership.

"Headship" is about the exercise of power by men over women, and has kept women "silent in the churches" and reinforced their sense of inferiority. Yet there is no agreement about the interpretation of the relevant texts. Rival exegeses were clearly set out by the Church of England Bishops in their Second Report in relation to the Ordination of Women (1988), but they could not reach a common mind. It is interesting to note that George Carey (later to become Archbishop of Canterbury), writing in 1984, made a strong case for maintaining "a proper balance between the finality of the Christian revelation as contained in Scripture and its openness to new possibilities in Christ". He added: "We have been slow to recognise the biblical testimony to the complementarity of men and women in Christian anthropology and have been reluctant to allow the Spirit's gifts to flow through women." Most women have no hesitation in rejecting the conservative reading of texts which would evermore maintain them in a subordinate role in church and community, whatever their abilities.

Sean Gill, writing of the Victorian period, says: "The Church of England was part of an increasingly powerful and self-confident middle-class world, whose definition of respectability was based upon a clear separation between the spheres of work and domesticity, and upon its ability to sustain a lifestyle in which women were above the necessity of undertaking paid employment." Of course, working-class women worked from necessity, but by the end of the 19th century they had been segregated into a small range of low-paid, low-status occupations. Most people, including working-class women, had accepted the domestic ideology.

Middle-class women could be frustrated by domestic constraints. They were lauded for their self-abnegation and devotion to family, but they gradually came to believe that they could share their gifts and skills from the domestic arena among the poor, and also those in need of moral guidance. (The purity of middle-class women was often compared with the laxity of the working classes.) Sean Gill continues: "Women seized the opportunities offered by the belief in the socially regenerative power of their unique religious and maternal attributes to undertake a wide range of philanthropic activities, ranging from the education of children to the reclamation of prostitutes."

These activities reflected the values of middle-class, Christian, Victorian society and they can be seen either as an outpouring of Christian mission or as a form of social control by the ruling class. In truth, there was something of both about them. Women formed the majority in church congregations and were engaged in parish work, such as district visiting and Sunday School teaching.

A few Christian women broke out of the constraints imposed by society, and made their voices heard in a wider arena, against considerable opposition. For example, Octavia Hill is remembered for her pioneering housing projects for the poor, and Florence Nightingale for her work in the field of health. A highly impressive campaigner of the period was Josephine Butler, whose campaign against the Contagious Diseases Acts of the 1860s made the public aware of the double standards of sexual morality. Although these were women of their time, they were not diverted from their mission by the patriarchal view of how women should behave. They were the exceptions.

The legacy of Victorian Christian restraints on women still remains in the community and the Church. Although independence of mind has become easier with each generation, many older women have been reluctant to upset their husbands, or the vicar, or the boss, by being too strident in their opinions or by claiming space to develop their own interests and skills. They dared not claim the metaphorical "Room of One's Own."

So exactly how have women in the 20th century begun to find their authentic voice through mission and community action? One answer can be found in voluntary work. A scheme which has acknowledged for 36 years the importance of women's volunteer pastoral work operates in Southwark Diocese in London. The Southwark Pastoral Auxiliaries (SPAs) scheme – described to me by Joanna Cox, lay training adviser – was innovative in that it combined authorised lay pastoral ministry with locally-based, part-time training. It was the brainchild of Cecilia Goodenough, lay missioner in the diocese, to whom it had become apparent that there was a need for more women to work in areas of social need, particularly "where no organised church work was being done. They would need the courage to enter institutions where there had been no one to pave the way, to make contact with groups of people who had no links with the church, and to be able to work largely unsupported by the church, which might have little understanding of their activity."

In 1961, the first SPAs were trained, and in due course their training and ministry were incorporated into diocesan structures. There are currently more than 150 SPAs currently involved in ministry, among whom a small but growing minority are men.

Many, but not all, work within their own parishes and some also carry out general parish duties, but an important part of their purpose is "representing the pastoral mission of the church in the wider community". SPAs are carefully selected and undergo 16 months of training on an evening/weekend/private study basis, plus 40 hours of visits and placements before commissioning. Some are employed and have only limited time for voluntary work; others work long hours in the projects they have chosen. These vary widely. In the early days, many worked with the homeless. Now, some tasks might be parish-related, such as baptism preparation, leading the bereavement team or doing pastoral work on a local estate; others could be away from the parish, such as membership of a prison or hospital chaplaincy team, or assisting a Christian voluntary organisation.

The Mothers' Union, founded by Mary Sumner in 1876, is

a second example of Christian women's voluntary work. As an international body with paid staff in addition to its members, it is very different from the SPA scheme. It has developed a wide brief over the years, while maintaining its central concern for the family. Indeed, it has now become a large mission organisation and has to be viewed in relation to its overall influence, as well as to the contribution made by and on behalf of its members. In 1996, it had 750,000 members worldwide, based in 59 countries. The Home membership is 141,112, with 5,443 branches. Its fund balances in December 1996 were over £4 million. That said, the Home membership is decreasing steadily, with only 9,751 members with children under 16, which suggests an ageing membership.

There is obviously a belief among British MU members about the need for renewal, which has led to the writing of a new Mission Statement (1996/97.) The emphasis is on developing spiritual growth in families, studying and reflecting on family life, and providing resources for members to take practical action to improve conditions for families. The level of practical help through grants, training and the voluntary work of members is impressive.

The organisation has a respected voice in national debate on issues to do with family life, whether in supporting moves to extend maternity leave to adoptive mothers, or producing a discussion paper on domestic violence. In the recent discussion on euthanasia, the national social policy officer produced a paper for discussion, which was sent out from the central committee to all members, with a questionnaire. Branches then held meetings on the topic, often bringing in expert speakers, and the ensuing debate was very vigorous. The MU was then able to express a public opinion with solid backing from a well-informed membership.

The MU in Southwark has worked with the South London Industrial Mission (SLIM) and with a number of companies in the London area. Seminars were set up to discuss "family-friendly" policies in the workplace. Papers were presented about changing work patterns, and about a project to help small businesses to enable their staff to balance effectively work and family life.

These endeavours belie the popular image of the MU as the "catering corps" of the Church. Although most women join it for companionship and support, and some groups are very low-key, women can find in an avenue for self-development and for making a contribution to the community. In addition, the organisation operates in a national and international arena, with more influence than its members could possibly manage alone. Perhaps the organisation's main challenge now is to recruit younger members to help in the modernisation process – people who will be more ready to challenge Church structures and who will understand the changing family.

What about the contribution of women employees of the Church, and their impact on Church and community? There was considerable opposition in the 19th century to the idea of women becoming full-time church workers, but in spite of this Anglican sisterhoods were revived in 1845 and the deaconess movement in 1861. But lay church workers, who followed the philanthropic ladies of an earlier period, increasingly needed training and pay. In 1919, the Inter-Diocesan Committee for Women's Work set out to co-ordinate women's church work and to provide certificated training. However, these dedicated women were often working for a starvation wage. For example, early annual reports of WelCare in Southwark Diocese (then called the Diocesan Association for the Care of Friendless Girls) describe "the grossly exhausting nature of Outdoor Work, its harsh effects on the women staff and the pitifully poor pay.... Small wonder that many of the workers suffered a breakdown in health. Yet there can be no doubt that these women, thrust into an alien environment – many were vicar's daughters and their like – worked with remarkable energy and conviction."

For many years to come, women continued to receive salaries substantially less than that of a curate, and without the accommodation – yet another way in which the Church discouraged and under-valued women's service. In 1960, the various committees co-ordinating women's work were merged into the Council for Women's Ministry in the Church, which provided a three-year training course. According to Gill: "In 1966, there were said to be 3,500 full-time church workers, of whom 78 were deaconesses, 307 lay workers, 222 Church Army sisters, 434 church social workers, and 2,658 professed religious."

Social and community work has been developed on a large scale in the secular sphere during the 20th century, forgetting its Christian origins. There are, however, still a number of important Christian social work agencies, such as the Children's

Society and Barnardo's, which have gradually changed their Victorian focus of providing homes for destitute children. For example, in addition to a range of pioneering projects for children and young people, the Children's Society now does a great deal of campaigning on behalf of children. On a smaller scale, some dioceses still have social work services: some are adoption agencies, some provide hostels for families in need.

WelCare is the service in Southwark Diocese. Its mission statement indicates that it "works alongside parents and young children in need to achieve a better quality of life for the family". Staff members are all qualified, in social work or child care, but there are also over 100 volunteers engaged in the work, and the trustees are all volunteers, too – mostly from the local church community. WelCare works with about 1,000 families in need at any one time in South London and East Surrey, providing a range of services: advice and advocacy, family social work; group work; practical help; outings and holidays. There is a range of specialist projects. In one branch, in addition to the core family work, there are five other projects, including one to help families affected by HIV/Aids, a project to provide play programmes for the children of the homeless, and a contact centre where children of divorced parents can meet with their non-custodial parent in a safe, child-friendly environment. The variety of local projects aims to meet local need as well as fitting the aims of the organisation.

Among the clientele, many are lone-parent families, whose numbers have greatly increased in the last two decades. Lone parents have had a bad press and there is relatively little sympathy for them in the wider community, although many are dealing with crushing problems. Offering a service to such families does not easily gain support – which is a strong reason for the Church to continue to include it in mission. Yet within the Church, a "women's organisation" is likely to lack influence, especially when budgets are being discussed (money is still very much an area of male influence).

An issue that arises in relation to much pastoral work, including that of WelCare, is whether the mission task includes evangelism. At a time of concern about falling numbers, the Church sometimes seems to lose touch with the most basic meaning of mission: "Serve Your Neighbour." Bishop Roy Williamson, the recently retired Bishop of Southwark, used to quote St. Francis: "Preach the gospel wherever you go, use words if you must." The bishop added: "Clearly St. Francis had discovered the power and influence of communication beyond language ... the Good News of God is revealed in actions that speak louder than words." People who know WelCare's work are aware of how often women and children who have been at the end of their tether gain confidence, hope and self-respect; how family relationships improve; and how people who have been seeking a sense of direction in their lives begin to find their way.

WelCare has struggled to escape its Victorian heritage of "doing good" to the poor. Its women clients are often inarticulate and powerless – or, at least, at their point of greatest need. Staff work alongside them, encouraging the women to be active in solving their own problems. For example, social workers may act as advocates, helping women to present a coherent case to the DSS or the housing authority, but the intention is to enable them to act on their own behalf in future. Women sometimes become involved in the development of the organisation, by joining user groups or acting as client representatives on committees. Some find a voice for the first time in wider society; they learn to negotiate first for themselves and then for others. Assistance to families is associated with concern about the unjust structures in society, and WelCare aims in a small way, through research or other means, to draw attention to family needs in the wider community.

The issue of women finding a voice was discussed when I met the diocesan community development adviser in Southwark, Ann Stricklen. In describing a piece of work in an inner-city area, she told how a church group decided on a community development project. It was an all-black group, all women and mostly young. "What was significant was what happened to those women in learning how to plan, how to get policy through, how to report to the PCC, how to get funding, how to budget and recruit. I remember the young woman who chaired the recruitment panel saying it had given her confidence to apply for internal promotion in her job. They blossomed into being a highly concerned, competent group, capable of policy-making. They were, in fact, ably supported by a woman incumbent, but the difference the planning process made to their confidence and skills was added value – beyond what will be achieved by the project worker. If you choose the right job for someone, it allows them to grow."

Before she died, early in 1999, Ann Stricklen discussed her concern with issues of participation, power and community – the individual contribution within the larger context, where, for historical reasons, women are always under-represented. She had become interested in other ways of including women than "token" representation on decision-making bodies. Exerting outside pressure for policy changes that take account of minorities is a way forward "while we are waiting to change the system". Women of minority ethnic groups and lesbian women have, of course, more than one agenda, and are even more likely to be under-represented. Ann believed that women should stand alongside other minorities in lobbying for change. She said: "We should acknowledge diversity and work together."

The process of women finding a voice has been most powerfully acted out during the campaign for the ordination of women. In the years after the first ordinations, what progress is being made, and what may women priests be able to offer the Church and community? All is not sweetness and light. The MSF survey of 1998, entitled "Are Anglican Priests being Bullied and Harassed?", had this to say: "Women have only recently been ordained, and though in 1992 the church settled a conflict which had threatened to break it apart, the long expressed hostility to female ordination by some elements within the church has still not disappeared. Within Ecclesiastical law, it is still perfectly acceptable to discriminate against women, where parochial Church Councils choose to pass the relevant motions to that effect. Second, clergy, at least according to the law, are not employees. They do not therefore have recourse to the employment protection legislation which women who suffer discrimination or harassment in the workplace can normally use.... Add to that a climate in which it is perceived by many women clergy to be difficult to gain secure positions (incumbencies), and the evidence of fear inhibiting them from speaking out, and the result is a mixture fraught with danger."

Well over a hundred responses from women were received from the survey, and of these 75 per cent had experienced problems – including verbal abuse, isolation, harassment and physical abuse. Extensive examples are given, and they make painful reading. Such experiences have also been recorded elsewhere. Alison Rollin's unpublished dissertation (undertaken for the University of Westminster) included 12 in-depth interviews with women priests. She wrote that "the degree of acceptance or rejection that the women received varied markedly, depending more on the tradition of their church than on geographical location or personal status. . . . Those women who endured relatively high levels of discrimination and verbal abuse experienced this mainly around the time of the Synod vote (in 1992) and up until their ordination; a few continued to suffer for some time afterwards."

Most of the women in Rollin's small survey, however, experienced support from family, friends and colleagues, including many in the Church. This was also the experience of the Rev. Bernice Broggio, one of the senior women clergy in Southwark Diocese. She believes that, although some women have experienced difficulties, most have been treated fairly and well. Her own career of 38 years is an interesting illustration of how women have reached the priesthood – involving, in her case, most of the aspects of women's ministry already explored in this chapter. It shows the determination, commitment and conviction about vocation that has brought women through the stress of the long campaign. From early on, these women found a strong voice in the Movement for the Ordination of Women, where they also experienced the importance of the mutual support which women offer each other in all walks of life.

It is still early days, and therefore impossible to make useful judgments about what contribution women will make through ordained ministry. The first generation of women priests have the advantage of bringing previous life experience in church and community to the task. Bernice draws upon her social work (pastoral) skills, her management experience and her knowledge of the workings of four previous parishes in her work as vicar and rural dean. Future women priests will continue to bring home and work experience to the job. It is widely accepted already that women have brought special gifts to funeral and marriage ministry, and that they are well established as chaplains in hospitals and prisons.

In 1994, the year of the first ordinations, a fascinating book called *Crossing the Boundary: What Will Women Priests Mean?* was published. It drew together a collection of essays speculating on women's contribution after ordination. Cathy Milford saw some positive outcomes of the long wait: "The waiters have been the gainers, gainers in that they have been able to discover and articulate that which lies below the surface of the struggle to ordain women as priests. The flowering of feminist theology, feminist spirituality and feminist liturgy bears this out."

Milford also reflected upon the "feminine". She wrote: "In our western society, woman has become the symbol of nurture and community.... I said before that I believed that both women and men carry feminine and masculine characteristics, and that to be fully human is to be able to use the full range of these characteristics. Having said that, within our society woman is the symbol of the feminine, and it seems to me that what is happening is that our society badly needs to recover the feminine, and that need has actually triggered the search and the revaluation in the church."

Una Kroll, in a contribution to the same book, wrote: "When I ask for ministry from a woman priest, deacon or laywoman, I expect to find in her . . . qualities that reflect the motherhood of God, the sisterhood of Christ and the close and warm friendship of the Holy Spirit. . . . " She expresses her hope that women priests would not "forsake their womanliness for the sake of conforming to an established male pattern of ordained ministry", but then goes on to say that when people are confident they can be comfortable with "the deeper complementary qualities" which exist in us all – the masculine and feminine integrated. The message here seems to be that women should be relaxed and believe in what they bring as women, not trying to move too fast from what they know, and having confidence that God wants a greater range of attributes brought to ministry.

Women's struggle to find their role in the Church and in the community is not so very different whether they be priests, lay workers, volunteers or ordinary citizens with no Christian allegiance. Over the centuries they have been tied to roles as housewives, mothers, wives and daughters, and have been restricted in education, employment, political life and under the law. The Church, as much as any other institution, has restricted and abused them – or placed them on a pedestal, which is almost as damaging. The extraordinary changes of the last century have allowed women freedoms and opportunities in Church and community beyond the wildest dreams of their

Victorian sisters.

Change is always difficult, and rapid change even more so. Neither men nor women yet feel wholly comfortable with the wider opportunities possessed by women. Women still suffer from guilt about conflicting roles, frustration about "glass ceilings", and anxiety when challenging men. Men continue to use their entrenched power to control female progress. Yet what has been achieved is extraordinary and should be celebrated. Women at last can use their God-given gifts at home, at work and in ministry, without the restrictions of the past. They can follow their calling in small ways and large. In due course, they and others will know what difference the women's voice will make in Church and community.

Denise Mumford is a retired social worker and former director of WelCare in Southwark Diocese, London.

Selected reading

Sean Gill *Women and the Church of England*, (SPCK, Great Britain. 1994).

Peter Hancock *WelCare Past, Present and Future (1894-1994)*, (available from Southwark Diocese).

Sue Walrond-Skinner, (Editor) *Crossing the Boundary*, (Mowbray, London. 1994. Ch. 4 and 10).

Chapter Twelve

Open and shut case: The asylum crisis

by Patrick Logan

The 1990s opened a new chapter in the response of British churches, particularly in London and the south-east, to the needs of asylum-seekers. Now that the government has begun putting in place its new proposals to disperse a minimum of 48,000 asylum-seekers, churches in the rest of Britain will also have to decide how they are going to respond. Prior to the 1990s, church involvement was limited to a relatively few, albeit excellent responses – the Ockenden Venture, the Jesuit Refugee Services, and, in London, the Westminster Diocese Refugee Service and local initiatives such as the Windmill Project and the Oaklands Project. In addition, some churches took more prophetic action, invoking ancient custom and offering their churches as places of sanctuary, as in the case of Viraj Mendis, who was felt to be faced with deportation that would put his life at risk.

The situation changed dramatically with the leap in asylum seekers from 4,256 applications a year in 1987 to 44,840 in 1991 and to nearly 60,000 in 1999. The speed and scale of churches' mobilisation in response to the plight of asylum-seekers since January 1996 is almost unprecedented. The ruthlessness of the cuts in income support and housing benefit, as well as the peremptory manner in which they were announced, ignited a flame of compassion and anger within congregations across London and elsewhere. But the churches' response was basically a crisis response, and crisis responses cannot continue indefinitely.

So the crisis itself looks set to continue. It is expected that in the next few years, well over one hundred new claims for asylum will be made each day. Even if the Home Office granted Exceptional Leave to Remain to some 30,000 of those who have been waiting years for a decision, this would still leave around 70,000 asylum-seekers without entitlement to social security, housing or other basic rights. By no means all will be at risk of destitution but a large proportion will be.

But even for the 25 per cent or so who, on present trends, will either be granted refugee status or given exceptional leave to remain, the struggle to rebuild their lives will not be easy. Mastering an unfamiliar language and adjusting to a strange climate may be the easiest bits. Much more painful is the humiliation that comes from the refusal to recognise one's skills and the requirement to have them revalidated. And most frightening of all is the unexpected, unprovoked and vicious racist attacks. The sense of insecurity, isolation and even alienation is not easily overcome.

Whatever the government does, like it or not, the need for Church involvement is bound to continue for the foreseeable future. Along with other voluntary agencies working with asylum-seekers, the churches are at a crossroads. How do they get beyond a crisis response? Having put their hand to the plough, the churches will not be so irresponsible as to let go and hope that others will take up where they have left off. But they may feel that it is just as irresponsible simply to go on ploughing the same furrow while other fields may prove more fertile. The question is not whether the churches should continue their work, but how.

Contrary to the myth propagated from some quarters, Britain is not the haven chosen above all others because of its soft entry controls and over-generous benefits system. The destabilisation that followed the collapse of Communist regimes in Europe and the withdrawal of super-power patronage to proxy regimes in Africa led to an explosion in the number of people seeking refuge in almost every part of Western Europe. The demons of xenophobia, racism and tribalism thus unleashed were as terrifying as they were uncontrollable. The response? "Fortress Europe".

In the UK, the first signs of a much tougher line came in July 1991 with a declaration by the then Home Secretary, Kenneth Baker. He was certainly correct in calling attention to the rapid rise in numbers of people then seeking asylum in Britain, but it was the tone of the announcement, as well as its proposals, which signalled that we were entering a new period. After the General Election of 1992 came the highly controversial Asylum and Immigration Appeals Act of 1993. Ironically, though the number of applicants for asylum had fallen before the Bill was published, the government had concluded that tougher measures were needed. One of these was a doubling in the use of detention.

But a broader wave of concern was already beginning to sweep through the churches – and, indeed, other faith communities. In June 1992 came the adoption of the formal constitution of Faith Asylum Refuge (FAR), a network whose aim was to encourage faith communities to make new efforts to extend hospitality to refugees and asylum-seekers. This network had the official backing of the leaders of most of the major faiths in the UK and was publicly launched in May 1993. Within months, the stage was being set for a new mobilisation.

The spark that lit the flame was a proposal at the Conservative Party Conference of 1995, when the then Social Security Minister, Peter Lilley, proposed without warning that thousands of asylum-seekers were to lose their entitlement to income support, housing benefit and council tax benefit. Anyone who applied for asylum from within the UK after 8 January 1996, and anyone who received a negative decision on their application after that date, even if they lodged an appeal, would no longer be entitled to such benefits. To stop in their tracks potential applicants already in the UK, Lilley added that anyone who applied for asylum from within the UK after the date of his announcement, and anyone who received a negative decision on their application after that date, even though they had lodged an appeal, would also have their benefits stopped as from 8 January. No Parliamentary debate was thought to be needed, though one was eventually demanded and granted. The implications were devastating. Without housing benefit, and with no other means to pay their rent, people would be homeless. And without income support, people could find themselves literally destitute, unable to buy even food or second-hand clothing.

How many people would be affected? The government said 13,000, but this failed to take account of the far greater number of people who might be expected to claim asylum from within the UK after 8 January 1996. "As many as 40,000 asylum seekers will be affected every year," warned the Refugee Council. Not all those affected would be people with no financial resources, but by August 1999 the number of asylum-seekers who had been denied benefit and who would have been destitute but for the emergency, non-cash assistance being given by London's local authorities was nearly 40,000. As though the withdrawal of benefits were not enough, additional measures barring asylum-seekers from housing and employment were drawn up in amendments to the Housing Bill and in the new Asylum and Immigration Bill, which were both given royal assent in July 1996.

The reaction of Church leaders to Lilley's moves was immediate. In December, the Bishop of Liverpool, together with the former President of the Methodist Conference, the Moderator of the Churches' Commission for Racial Justice and a spokesperson for the Council of African and Afro-Caribbean Churches, wrote a letter of protest to *The Times*. The London Churches Group urged London's church leaders to alert their members to the crisis.

Existing Christian agencies and networks sprang into action. Family agencies such as WelCare, single homelessness day centres like Providence Row and residential providers like the Salvation Army, parish-based charities such as the Society of St. Vincent de Paul, and networks such as Justice and Peace groups and the Catholic Women's League all sought to adapt their services to address the needs of asylum-seekers. And action was taken by individual church leaders, including the bishops of Rochester and Aston, who offered to stand bail for asylum-seekers who would otherwise have been detained in prison.

But the most significant development was the emergence of the Inter-faith Refugee Network. A joint appeal by the London Churches Group and by Westminster Social and Pastoral Action led to well over 100 people turning up for two training days in early 1996. Thus was born the Ecumenical Refugee Network, which, in the autumn of that year, changed its name to the Inter-faith Refugee Network (IRN). Within months, thanks to the encouragement and support of the IRN, new ecumenical action groups were up and running in two-thirds of the 32 London boroughs. What made these spontaneous local initiatives all the more remarkable was the fact that, for the most part, they were not simply extensions of existing church projects but were entirely new groupings, bringing together people from churches which previously had not worked together – evangelical, Catholic, community churches, free churches. With virtually no previous experience, with the flimsiest of infrastructure and with precious little money, these local groups appeared almost overnight.

What they offered above all was immediate, practical help and support to people who were threatened with destitution – food, clothing, furniture, transport, help with language, advocacy on the few rights to assistance that did remain, such as health care and social services. In many areas, local churches made their own premises available for such services, even where these services were being offered by refugee groups or by the Refugee Council.

From the beginning, the churches recognised that they could never hope to provide a substitute for the withdrawal of social security and housing for 40,000 or more people. The only way forward was close collaboration with other voluntary agencies, particularly the Refugee Council, with refugee community forums, with other faith groups, particularly J-Core (Jewish Council for Racial Equality), and with local authorities. At the policy and planning level, this led the churches to work with the wider voluntary sector and with local authorities in producing a report called "Towards a Co-ordinated Strategy", as early as June 1996. At a practical level, this meant working with local authorities in their use of the 1948 National Assistance Act to provide help to asylum-seekers. But the extent of such assistance was woefully inadequate.

The policy of local authorities was inconsistent, as was their interpretation of what the law did or did not permit them to offer. Because they could not give cash payments, the result was a highly complicated and costly system of vouchers, requiring repeated visits to and assessment by local authorities, as well as the lack of choice which cash payments would have made possible. Local authorities resented the whole arrangement, claiming that the reimbursement they receive from the Department of Health was less than the expense involved and that, more fundamentally, it was central government rather than local authorities which should be providing such help. In short, conditions were hardly favourable for an effective, long-term partnership.

In suddenly providing services free of charge to asylum-seekers, the churches were running a double risk of being exploited – a risk which grew the more the churches were applauded for their splendid efforts. From one direction, there was the risk of being exploited by central government and local authorities. What could be more convenient for statutory bodies than to discover that people they might otherwise be required to help were being provided for so much more cheaply by local church groups, or for that matter by friends? The authorities could, and in some cases did, go one step further, arguing that as long as an asylum-seeker was receiving help of this sort they had no further claim to statutory assistance. From the opposite direction, there was the risk of being exploited by individuals whose grounds for claiming asylum were very flimsy indeed. Far outweighing this risk, however, was the very real consideration that such people are often none the less facing severe hardships.

Both these forms of exploitation did happen. And the churches were not so naive as to fail to realise the fact. But they also realised that were they to stop offering help, tens of thousands of asylum-seekers could face destitution and despair. The churches were being placed in a position that should not and could not continue indefinitely. Sooner or later, under-resourced and largely volunteer-run local church groups would simply collapse from exhaustion. What began as a valiant effort could all too easily end in the depths of failure and guilt.

Throughout their involvement, the churches have never lost sight of the overriding need to press governments, Conservative and Labour, for more just policies towards asylum-seekers. The late Cardinal Hume, in his address at the opening of an emergency night shelter hastily set up by the Refugee Council, said forthrightly: "Asylum-seekers are not popular. They easily arouse hostility and resentment. . . . They make a useful scapegoat for those who wish to appeal only to people's self-interest or who promote a narrow nationalism." The churches held top-level meetings with ministers on several occasions, and bishops used their place in the House of Lords to press for amendments to government legislation. In this struggle for justice, one of the most influential church bodies has been the Churches Refugee Network, part of the Council of Churches for Britain and Ireland's Commission on Racial Justice.

But questions of justice are rarely simple. The churches' struggle for justice for asylum-seekers began where it should – not with some academic or legalistic debate but by standing alongside and sharing the trials of those who have fled their native land. And this is where the churches must continue to take their stand for justice. At the same time, this cannot be an excuse for a self-righteous refusal to face up to some of the awkward facts that bedevil even the best-intentioned Christian legislators. There are, for example, thousands of people seeking asylum who come from countries where there is certainly no *prima facie* case for suspecting that the claims would have a solid basis. This is not to justify the devising of a "White List" of supposedly untroubled countries, which is then used to reject claims simply on the basis of where a person happens to come from rather than on their individual circumstances. It is to the government's credit that its White Paper promises to end the use of a "White List".

But neither is it responsible for Christians to try to minimise the extent of asylum abuse. There is the further difficulty arising from the fact that there are limits to the number of asylum-seekers Britain can accept, even allowing for the fact that asylum-seekers' reasons for flight are normally temporary and the desire to return home when the situation has improved is generally very strong. Certainly in London there is enormous pressure on virtually all forms of accommodation – except on hard-to-let council estates, which may hardly be the place to refer someone who is seeking asylum. Christians do not make their cause more credible by appearing not even to recognise, much less to offer solutions to, the problem of limits.

The churches have brought their experiences with asylum-seekers, and their struggles for justice on their behalf, into their life of prayer and worship. This is true not just in the services held regularly in local churches. There have also been higher profile events as well. In Holy Week, 1996, a number of Christian organisations held a moving "Refugee Way of the Cross" on the streets of central London. In early 1997, the Southwark Diocesan Board for Church in Society put together a powerful photographic exhibition that was first displayed in Southwark Cathedral and then in other London churches. Innumerable local churches have been holding their own vigils.

Looking ahead, it seems that the New World Order has proved to be unstable, unequal and unjust. In spite of the best efforts of international agencies, peace and development will not come quickly. Meanwhile, millions of people will be driven to seek safety and improvement in safer, more economically active countries. Whether as refugees or migrant workers, the

143

overwhelming majority will continue to make their way to other countries in the developing world. But a significant number will continue to seek a haven in Western European countries, and in many cases will do so by claiming asylum. It is increasingly clear that the concerted response of European Union governments is to tighten up their laws and procedures on immigration and asylum-seeking. The fact that most of these governments are centre or (mildly) left-of-centre politically, and that they are managing to keep ugly rightwing forces at bay, is of small comfort.

Any hope that a Labour government might reverse the harsh measures introduced by the previous Conservative government is proving unfounded. Deterrence seems to be the underlying aim of the government's 1999 Immigration and Asylum Act. Its two-pronged attack is aimed, first, at making it harder for potential asylum-seekers to enter the UK and, secondly, to make life more insecure for those who do apply for asylum. The safety net provided by the National Assistance Act will no longer apply to asylum-seekers and a whole host of statutory duties previously incumbent on local authorities will be removed. Support will be available principally through a new Asylum Support Directorate, run by and in accordance with Home Office policy dictates and endowed with discretionary powers. There are widespread fears that the result will be to increase the social exclusion of asylum-seekers, most of whom could live in destitution on a scale unknown for generations.

The churches will be part of this new scenario and are, not surprisingly, faced with a dilemma. Some fear that the clear message is that the churches will be expected to play a residual role, providing low-level emergency support for those who fall through the net. For that reason, some church groups are already saying that they simply will not play that sort of game. Others, whilst still resisting the pressure to play a residual role, are fighting to ensure that they can play a complementary role, i.e. working alongside rather than in place of statutory services, particularly those offered by local authorities. But even if the churches do manage to position themselves to play a complementary role, they will still need to be clearer about their role. Is it primarily about providing services (the "project" or "service" model), or is it primarily about helping people to resettle and integrate (the "community work" model)?

If we were starting with a clean slate, it might be argued that the case for adopting a community work model might most appropriately draw upon the best strengths of the church – that is, its commitment to the life of the local community and its awareness of the range of formal and informal resources that are there to be drawn upon and developed. But we are not starting with a clean slate. Many churches are already providing a social service that people have come to depend upon and which may not be lightly shut down. In any case, there is no general answer. Each local network will have to answer the question in its own way. The response that is right for one local church or group of churches may be wrong for another. The important thing is that the question be addressed. An important resource is the Inter-faith Refugee Network (IRN). Having kept in touch with the ups, downs and various turns of local church agencies, as well as having good links with national refugee agencies, IRN is ideally placed to help local churches to look responsibly to the next stage of their work – or, if need be, the winding down of their work.

For those churches wishing to adopt a community work model, there will be a further set of questions that will need to be addressed. What scope is there for working with asylum-seekers themselves as communities, rather than simply as individual cases? What are the possibilities for collective empowerment? What can be done to help prevent a refugee community from becoming isolated from the wider community? How best can we ensure that one faction or interest group does not dominate? How can we clarify who has the authority to do what and who is accountable to whom? These may be new questions for some churches. But they are not new for refugee communities or for the Refugee Council, which has for some time been working at this level and has been drawing on the experience of some of the churches' own community development expertise, such as that of the Southwark Diocesan Board for Church in Society.

For churches wishing to develop their social service role, a different set of questions will need to be addressed. Precisely what kind of service do they want to offer (advice, counselling, skills-training, etc)? Who decides which service is most needed in a particular area and who is best placed to provide that service (it may not be the churches, but churches may help get that service established)? What structure of management is most appropriate for the service? What level of resourcing is needed (staff as well as funding), where will it come from and what strings will be attached? What will resourcing seek to achieve, and how will it be monitored? The churches ought not to address these questions on their own. Consultation with the local community is important, as are effective links with providers of complementary services such as housing, health care, education and training.

There is a very real danger that churches may feel pressured to assume functions that are more appropriately carried out by central government (providing social security benefits) and by local government (providing care and accommodation). Alongside proposals for a new national mechanism that would provide "in-kind" (that is, non-cash) assistance to asylum-seekers there is a radical cutback of the role of central and local government. In this scenario, churches will be pushed into assuming a role that will often be quite inappropriate. The crunch question is: To what extent will churches refuse to be part of such a game, and to what extent will they feel their refusal to play will cause even greater hardship to asylum-seekers?

The issue of asylum-seekers in Britain needs constantly to be set within the wider global context. Questions of human rights and economic justice are more pressing than ever, given the absence of democratic and welfare infrastructures in so many parts of the world and given the economic forces which, in many cases, actually impeded the formation of such structures. And placing the issue in terms of justice means spelling out how, in many cases, it is the economic and political priorities of the Western world which have contributed to the dislocation elsewhere.

Campaigns like Jubilee 2000, and its counterparts in other European countries, for the remission of debt for the poorest countries show that it is possible to catch the imagination of millions of our fellow citizens. The advent of the new millennium must be a time to get beyond the endless crisis-intervention and into radical social transformation. Many in the churches are well along that path and many have been greatly helped in their work for justice by the Churches Refugee Network, which has helped to remind the Church that, as well as being grounded in the local community, the Church is also a universal body with a universal mission.

In struggling with the various and conflicting pressures and opportunities open to them in responding to the needs of asylum-seekers, the churches' most fundamental concern must be to respond as church. It means evangelising – proclaiming the good news to the poor – without necessarily proselytising. It means being pastoral – holding on to and developing its caring role. It means being prophetic – demanding justice from the powerful. These roles are dimensions of the Church's mission, not alternatives, and all of them need constantly to be grounded in and expressed in private and shared prayer for strength and discernment.

An excellent example of how it is possible to work in this highly pressurised sector, without losing sight of one's proper identity and role as a church, is the Jesuit Refugee Service. Precisely because of its growing significance in working with refugees, the JRS was invited to move its headquarters to Geneva, where it might have become a more integral part of the global NGO network. What was presented as an opportunity was rightly perceived as a temptation, and the offer was turned down. What JRS valued above all else was its specifically Christian identity and the freedom that went with it. Rather than gain a place nearer the head table, it insisted on keeping its place with refugees, thus reaffirming its commitment "to be with" rather than "to do for". The continuing proof of the wisdom of this choice can be seen in the regular reports JRS provides in its newsletter and in the prominence given to the spiritual dimensions of their work, as seen in publications such as *Keeping Hope Alive.*

As we try to make sense of our future and our past at the beginning of a new millennium, the issue of asylum-seekers takes on an added significance. It is not just a matter of responding to a crisis but of realising that the future of our planet depends upon the deepening of the sense of being and of behaving as one human family. The churches' continued involvement with asylum-seekers is a vital witness to that belief.

Dr Patrick Logan is housing and homelessness adviser for the Diocese of Southwark.

Chapter Thirteen
Raising the roofs: Homes and the homeless

by Niall Cooper

"A home is more than having a roof over one's head. Decent housing certainly means a place that is dry and warm and in reasonable repair. It also means security, privacy, sufficient space, a place where people can grow and make choices.... To believe that you have no control over one of the most basic areas of your life is to feel devalued."

These words are taken from *Faith in the City*, the report of the Archbishop of Canterbury's Commission on urban priority areas, published in 1987, and they still represent an appropriate starting point for a Church response to problems of housing need and homelessness.

In other words, to have a house and home is the bedrock of participation in society and community. The Christian churches attribute a fundamental value to housing. The need for shelter and settlement is recognised in Christian teaching as a necessary precondition to the growth and fulfilment of human beings made in the image of God. Yet the paradox of housing is that it is both builder and destroyer of community. Housing brings us together in communities, but at the same time can do more to set us apart than almost any other aspect of our lives. In a society riven by division between rich and poor, how we are housed (or not) has profound consequences not simply for our physical place of abode, but for social location and life experience.

Housing policy has been one of the major causes of social polarisation in Britain, not just for the past 15 years but for 50 and more. Preoccupied with its own concerns for fluctuating mortgage rates and house price inflation, home-owning Middle England has become blind to the iniquities meted out to the other nation of private and council tenants, plus a population the size of Leeds who experience what it is to be without a home each year. It is an indictment of society that homelessness has always been an accepted – if not acceptable – part of the landscape. "Men of the road" (tramps or vagrants, depending on your turn of phrase) have always been objects of pity but not of obligation. Yet single people and childless couples are still afforded no legal right to a roof over their heads.

As a result, in the last 10 years we have permitted the growth of an entirely new phenomenon (certainly in this century): the emergence of large-scale youth homelessness. Mass youth unemployment, successive cuts in benefit levels (and their abolition for 16 and 17 year olds), and the mass privatisation of council housing has cast thousands of young single people into a state of homelessness, lacking not only any right to a home, but in many cases to the right to financial assistance from the state.

The numbers visibly homeless – hanging around, sleeping, begging or, more latterly, selling the *Big Issue* magazine – has mushroomed in the last decade. The numbers who are invisibly homeless – sleeping on friends' floors, "skipping" in derelict buildings, or filling to overflowing the hostels and night shelters which have sprung up in almost every town and city across the country – is far, far greater. Most worryingly, agencies have reported a dramatic increase in the numbers of 16 and 17 year olds (and younger) who are becoming homeless. Yet, since successive governments have not seen fit even to count the numbers of those affected, there are no reliable statistics as to the number of young and single people who have experienced homelessness over the last 10 years. By the best estimates, the number is certain to be counted in the hundreds of thousands. But the real scandal is not simply the numbers affected, or the individual hardship caused, but the fact that the situation is largely of our own making.

In the words of Nick Hardwick, former director of Centrepoint Soho, in London, "Young people sleep on the streets not because of some Act of God or personal inadequacy but because that is how we as a society choose to organise things."

Even those to whom society affords some legal protection face a pretty raw deal. The 1976 Homeless Persons Act was a watershed in creating limited right to housing for the "deserving poor" – families, vulnerable people and elderly people. Despite a weakening of its provisions by subsequent legislation, local authorities remain obliged to ensure that those unintentionally homeless people who fall into such "priority" categories are provided with a roof over their heads. This remains a key factor in why so few families with children end up visibly homeless on our streets.

Yet homeless families are frequently consigned to a twilight existence of temporary accommodation, bed and breakfast hotels and the like. More than 44,300 families were living in temporary accommodation at the end of 1997. This represents a miserable and unsettling experience for many families. There is a widely-held view that the households that do get placed in temporary accommodation will normally survive without too much damage because it is only for a short period. However, for many the reality is different. Despite the term "temporary", this is an existence that has to be endured for anything from a couple of weeks to a matter of years, with little guarantee of what sort of housing they will be offered at the end of it. It can result in separation from friends and family networks, the loss of employment, interrupted schooling for children, disrupted health care, severance of contact with a GP, and the undermining of relationships and trust within families.

For Nila – married with three young children - and thousands of families like hers, the consequences of redundancy, poverty, debt, mortgage arrears and finally homelessness have been devastating. At the National Poverty Hearing, held in March 1996, she declared: "Eventually the building society repossessed the house, and we found ourselves at the mercy of the housing department. On the morning we were due to move, I sent my son to school as normal. He asked me where we would be sleeping that night and I had no answer to give. We had been through rough times before. I had always had an answer, and explanation. I had never lied to him. The look in his eyes as he refused to look into mine haunts me still."

Re-housing can offer little salvation, since social housing has become increasingly ghettoised. Five million people now live in some 2,000 large estates where the average income is below the European poverty line. Research has shown that the rise in joblessness in the 1980s was concentrated almost exclusively among the tenants of councils and housing associations, leading to a qualitatively different experience, where poverty and unemployment have now become the norm rather than the exception on many estates. The rise in crime throughout the 1980s was also concentrated in the same areas, but has also been largely ignored. While the rest of us have suffered from the fear of crime and unemployment, that other nation knows the harsh realities at first hand.

Housing associations are now recreating the same segregation and marginalisation as their municipal predecessors. Financial pressures have led to rising rents and falling standards – and a desperate poverty trap for the vast majority of new tenants. Three out of four new housing association tenants now have no earned income, and those that do can loose more than 97 pence of every extra pound that they earn, through tax, national insurance and loss of benefits. Space standards have been squeezed to such an extent that in two-thirds of new association properties the family does not even have enough room to sit down and eat together.

All this has come about as the predictable outcome of housing allocations systems and government policy over a decade or more. At the root the problem is a systematic undermining of the option to rent, typified by the fact that in recent years, local councils and housing associations have built fewer new affordable homes to rent than at any time since 1945.

Little of this has happened entirely by accident. It is the result of a series of quite deliberate policy choices – to reduce benefit levels, to cut back on public investment in housing, to sell of over a million of the best council houses at knockdown prices. It is tempting, but ultimately unsatisfactory, to heap all the blame for this on 18 years of failed Conservative housing policies. But it is more disturbing to ponder our own complicity in the situation: that the current fault line between the well housed and the badly housed and unhoused is a direct, if unintended, consequence of our own deepest desires and aspirations for security and a "comfortable life".

The 30 per cent of the population without the financial means to buy their way into the housing market have little or no choice of where they live. Excluded from the so-called property-owning democracy, they are forced to rely on the vagaries (and expense) of the private rented market, or the lottery of council or housing association allocation systems. They have neither choice over the neighbourhood in which they end up, nor of the neighbours with whom they are required to "build community".

The inequalities of power, financial muscle and social influence that affect such communities are therefore hardly accidental. Communities of the poor are expected to bear an unequal share of society's "problems" precisely because communities of the better-off are much more successful in keeping them at arm's length. To this extent, Nimbyism ("We don't want those undesirable types in our back yard . . .") is only the more vulgar face of more deeply-ingrained and widely-shared attitudes enshrined in current housing and planning policy.

Yet there is a limit to the extent to which we can inure ourselves and cut ourselves off from the realities of poverty and consequences of such huge social divisions by creating "our own little Edens". It is nowhere more clearly demonstrated than in the USA that ghettoising the poor into neighbourhoods cut off from the rest of society creates enormous problems that no government can control and generates a spiral of violence which attacks the whole community.

So how can the churches respond to the challenges thrown up by homelessness and housing division? Churches have a long tradition of serving on the front line, binding up the broken hearted, often where the open sores most irritate and offend. They have been pioneers of so many responses – from medieval almshouses, through the 19th-century housing developments of Octavia Hill, and the work of the Salvation Army, to the establishment of myriad local housing associations, day centres, night shelters, soup runs and rent/guarantee schemes in the past 25 years. According to one survey, up to a third of all voluntary housing projects have their roots in the Church, or the endeavours of individual Christians.

A national survey of day centres for homeless people, published in 1992, concluded: "The philosophy of many day centres is rooted in Victorian Christian values, and a wide range of denominations are involved in providing services to single homeless people. These values present an ideal of family and community that is at odds with contemporary reality. As one user pointed out, Christ himself was a single homeless man whose lifestyle could be seen as far from conventional. He would surely have been unhappy that the myths about family and community are most evident at Christmas time, when the media inevitably includes copy on the plight of street homeless people. Christmas serves as a reminder of the ideal community in which we do not live, and of the narrow interpretations that restrict our choices as people."

And yet, as in so many such endeavours, the reality is more complex. The strength of the churches' voluntary involvement in seeking to address housing need has also in many ways been its weakness. The impulse to act frequently comes from church groups or individuals wishing to "do something" about the perceived or real problem most visibly apparent around them. Such an impulse does not always lead to the most appropriate response.

I once received a letter from a vicar, in a town on the outskirts of London, whose action group had been fired up to "do something about homelessness in the town" by opening a night shelter. Having got some months down the road, the group had now discovered that there were not actually enough people sleeping rough to justify opening the night shelter, and were looking to me to "find them" some homeless people from elsewhere to justify their endeavours.

Today, the impulse behind many soup runs, night shelters, hostels and day centres is to be found in the Christian concepts of hospitality and sanctuary. Typically, a church crypt or hall would be located, with volunteers from the local church mobilised to collect donations, food and clothing. Draughty, damp and overcrowded, church crypts may be a stop-gap measure of last resort, but cannot be justified as a long-term response to the needs of homeless people "made in the image of God".

Many projects have of course moved on from small, voluntary beginnings to become major providers of resettlement, advice, support and all kinds of specialist work – from art therapy to accessing health and other mainstream welfare services. They provide a professional level of services to their clients – in the best sense of the word – that homeless people deserve nothing but the best quality and standard of provision.

But there remains a nagging impression that some church projects continue to assert that voluntary (and amateur) is best. The national day centres survey found that many church projects continue to offer very basic services – to a predominantly white and male clientele – rooted in a passive and philanthropic attitude that "homeless people were the passive recipients of hand-outs from urban missionaries". Churches have been known to insist on clients "praying for their food", or to impose restrictive moral standards which undermine their own ability to address issues of drugs or sexual health in a realistic "streetwise" way.

At worst, the culture of "anything is better than nothing" undermines the process of developing higher standards of accommodation and provision. There are stories, possibly apocryphal, about hostels run by people who have no interest in resettling their users because it would call into question their own existence, or of soup runs engaging in cut-throat competition to serve up tea and sandwiches to "their" clients. The depressing conclusion of the day centres' researcher was that "change is slow, and often where one group of people make a commitment to change and closure, there is another group – very often church based – ready to respond pragmatically and open another substandard service or institution".

At another level, churches sometimes are open to the accusation of being more concerned with philanthropic first aid work than being agents of long-term change. Ken Bartlett, is an Anglican priest who has spent his life working in housing, from helping to found the Paddington Churches Housing Trust in 1963, and chairing the board of Shelter, through to the lofty heights of assistant chief executive of the Housing Corporation. Reflecting on this experience, in an article for *Christian Action Journal* in 1995, he asked serious questions about whether the churches are guilty of colluding with injustice. "The danger for the church's work in society," he wrote, "is that we accept pagan agendas and try to make them less oppressive, rather than challenging those agendas and trying to replace them with the vision and values of Christ.... As a result, the church offers people not hope, but survival; it ceases to be a prophetic body and becomes the fifth emergency service – after fire, police, ambulance and the AA."

It is certainly true that empowerment has yet to become part of the lexicon of most church housing projects. In an interesting reversal of the usual direction of "exchange visits", two homeless activists from Sao Paulo, Brazil, spent a fortnight visiting church homelessness projects in London during the summer of 1996. What they found was that, unlike in Sao Paulo, the churches in

London, with a few notable exceptions, were using a social work model in which homeless people tended to be seen as recipients rather than as partners.

The challenge they left with London's church projects was not so much to get homeless people to accept responsibility for their plight, as for the projects to work with homeless people in the changing of society. One of the visitors, Maria Antonieta da Costa Viera, observed in 1996 that "the Christian commitment would be to assume the prophetic mission of announcing a new way of life and accepting the goal of participation in the transformation of an unjust world into a friendly community".

And yet when the Church does get itself organised to address issues of "structural injustice", it continues to reveal its potency as a lobbying force. In 1992, the Churches National Housing Coalition organised the first churches lobby of parliament on housing and homelessness. In little over six months, and with minimal resources, 3,000 people were mobilised to travel to Westminster, and more than half of all members of parliament were lobbied by organised delegations of local church members, project workers and homeless people. A total of 125 MPs signed up to an Early Day Motion "supporting the Coalition's contention that the growth and persistence of homelessness and bad housing is a matter of grave concern ... and further supports the Coalition's call for greater public and private investment in the provision of affordable rented housing".

The churches are blessed with a huge variety of resources that can be deployed in the struggle to build community in spite of the twin challenges of homelessness and housing need. Yet there continues to be a massive mismatch between the response of individual Christians and the response of the churches as institutions to the needs of the poor.

So often, when one scratches below the surface, much of the churches' engagement in work on housing and homelessness actually comes down to the work of small bands of heroic individuals – social entrepreneurs, in the contemporary jargon. A survey of church housing projects in the early 1990s found that many projects and housing workers felt a distinct lack of support from the Church.

To be sure, many church leaders and denominations have issued fine and strongly-worded statements on homelessness and housing need. From the Archbishop of Canterbury and the late Cardinal Hume down, church leaders have spoken up about the "sin" of homelessness and the failure of government to respond adequately to the scale of the problem. The problem is not one of ill will, but of institutional inertia and an unresolved clash of cultures and priorities. I'm talking here principally about how churches choose to use and administer their own historic assets of land, property and finance.

The churches own property in most of the towns and villages across our country, and as a result are continually making decisions about the development and sale of land, often in key positions. The way in which such decisions are made can be a powerful and highly visible sign to the wider community of the churches' own priorities. When redundant churches or housing is left empty for years on end, or sold off for luxury housing rather than to provide for the most needy in society, it can easily serve to contradict or undermine all our talk about solidarity with the poor and the marginalised.

To be sure, much church property is impossible to develop, or is so constrained by the requirements of charity law that the only uses to which it can be put offer no help at all to people who are homeless or in acute housing need. But church authorities cannot be absolved of any moral responsibility for the way in which they deploy or dispose of their assets. In the words of the Archbishop of Canterbury, "The (Churches National Housing) Coalition is right to suggest that the Churches need to look to their own responsibilities in this field. The message of the Coalition needs to come to us as Christians. We are not lecturing the rest of society – we are preaching to ourselves!"

Churches have to accept responsibility for the actions of those who administer their assets, as well as balancing the tension between the need to generate funds to pay clergy stipends and other commitments with the wider needs of the communities in which they are set. For too long, church authorities have hidden behind a smokescreen of legal obligations and a narrow view of religion – in the case of the Church Commissioners, quaintly couched in terms of the "cure of souls" – in which meeting basic (material) human needs is not considered to be part of the core activity of the church. In a depressingly high percentage of churches, property and finance decisions are governed more by secular commercial logic, and a desire to achieve the maximum return, than by wider considerations of mission and spiritual or moral duty.

Yet, with creativity and bold thinking, it is possible to turn a situation of potential conflict between the needs of church and community into an opportunity for mutual benefit. In the early 1990s, the Welsh Presbyterian Church, for example, adopted a radical approach to the use of its stock of redundant or surplus chapel buildings for affordable housing, as part of a wider strategy of partnership and renewal. Its Strategy for the Future has been an explicit attempt to release the capital and resources tied up in hundreds of semi-redundant ecclesiastical buildings, by encouraging the formation of one centre for worship and mission in each community in Wales. And central to the strategy was the establishment of Aelwyd Housing Association to purchase and develop redundant chapels for the provision of housing for the elderly, the homeless and young people, and to address the increasing shortage of affordable housing for local people in so many Welsh communities as properties are bought up by wealthy "incomers" as holiday and retirement homes. This was backed up by a £250,000 low interest loan from the church to Aelwyd to enable rents to be set at a lower rate than would otherwise have been possible.

In a similar vein, churches – and individual church members – need to give far more thought to the issue of where they invest. While the Church Commissioners are by far the largest church investment body, managing over £3.5 billion worth of investments, most churches, individually or collectively, are sitting on investments and pension funds running into tens of millions of pounds. The vast majority of such investments are treated as purely commercial operations, invested to secure the highest return – provided it is not made too grubby by association with areas of "negative" ethical concern, such as weapons manufacture, gambling, booze or fags. Can the Church think of nothing more positive to do with such a massive resource?

It is surely time that the churches sought to put their money where their mouth is and use their role as major financial institutions to more creative effect. In recent years, new mechanisms have been established which enable the safe investment of funds directly into social housing projects – and to receive a reasonable rate of return. Both the Quakers and the Churches National Housing Coalition have signed partnership deals with Triodos bank – a small, Dutch-based ethical bank – to establish Social Housing Accounts to encourage individual and institutional church investment into church-linked housing schemes. Whilst almost £3 million has been invested to date, this remains chicken feed compared with the sums of money that churches continue to invest in commercial property developments and multinational corporations across the world.

The most profound challenge facing both the Church and the wider community, however, is about how to reverse the divisions between the well housed and the badly housed and unhoused – divisions which have been built up and set in concrete, bricks and mortar by 50 years and more of divisive housing and planning policies.

In this task, we must be careful not to throw the baby out with the bath water. Social housing – housing provided by local authorities and housing associations – has been much maligned in recent years. In the public mind, the council estate has become a symbol of failure and a synonym for crime, drug dealing, vandalism and "babies on benefit". To be sure, local authorities have made huge mistakes in the way they have built and managed public housing. Yet what is the alternative? Third world-style shanty towns? US-style ghettos? In the considered view of the American economist J.K. Galbraith, "In no country does the market system provide good low-cost housing. This is a matter of prime importance and must everywhere be a public responsibility. Few things are more visibly at odds with the good society than badly housed or homeless people."

The problem we now face is a loss of confidence in social housing which has resulted in long-term under-investment, stigmatisation and geographical separation. At the political level, it is essential that we rediscover the will to invest adequately in the provision of decent housing for those without the financial wherewithal to do so for themselves. All civilised countries do so. But, at the same time, we must find ways to rebuild a common sense of community, within and between the well housed, badly housed and unhoused.

The Church surely cannot hope to solve this problem on its own. We must look to stimulate a culture change in social attitudes to housing, neighbourhood and community, and paradigm shift in government policy. Part of this must involve a willingness to confront the Nimby factor head on, and to take much more radical action to break up the ghettos of the well-heeled and well-housed from which the poor are excluded . At the same time, there must be a rebuilding of the ghettos to which the poor and marginalised are currently consigned.

What is required is the rediscovery of social solidarity between rich and poor communities. But, in attempting to heal the divide, the Church does have a theoretical advantage, in the form of its local neighbourhood base. This is not so much to be found in the increasingly flimsy Anglican claim that the parish church, by definition, in some way "services" the whole community, but in the existence of church congregations and workers (clergy and lay, paid and voluntary) within virtually every community, neighbourhood and estate across the country. No other social institution or movement can make such a claim. However, it is important not to overstate this claim.

The Church is in an ideal position to be an agent of change because of its independent nature, because it has access to resources that other organisations do not and because the very nature of its witness demands it to be a fellowship of people who sit with others, hear their stories and support them in their struggles. However, this is a difficult message to get across both to the Church, which sees itself as respectable and not wanting to taint itself with politics on a local level, and to people in the community, who see the churches as a patronising agency, ready to play Lady Bountiful but not ready to enter into their real situations

In many cases churches may be physically located in "Britain's dangerous places", but in terms of their social and cultural location, the clergy and congregation might as well be a million miles away. Many inner-city churches, far from facing up to the realities of poverty and poor housing all around them, become locked into a kind of a siege mentality.

One church in Manchester, with which I worked closely in the late 1980s, had barely attracted a single new member in the previous 20 years, since the estate on which it was located had been totally redeveloped. The vast majority of the congregation no longer lived in the area, and viewed the current population of the estate with immense suspicion, if not hostility, as unwashed, ungodly, benefit scroungers and ne'er do wells. Yet, with the backing of a minority of supportive members, funding from the Methodist Circuit and a certain amount of railroading from the minister, a furniture recycling project, café and drop-in centre was opened up. The project rapidly developed into an important community resource, providing cheap furniture to tenants moving into the newly-built housing association properties across the road from the church – people who would otherwise, in many cases, have had little more than a mattress to their name.

This illustrates the point that the churches retain a strategic location and the kind of resources that most other community groups operating in the same neighbourhoods would give their eye teeth for – property assets, human resources, a reliable (if declining) source of external funding, and the ability to develop and exploit networks which connect such neighbourhoods with potential partners and allies deep into suburbia.

Given such circumstances, churches must take their role and ability to be builders of community much more seriously. Housing is not simply to be viewed as a problem to be left to the experts to sort out, but as a key to the regeneration of community. Housing has a key role in putting the heart back into demoralised, impoverished and excluded communities.

After too many years in which housing has simply been viewed as a bricks and mortar issue, some churches and housing agencies are beginning to wake up to this fact. For housing providers, this means a new and wider responsibility, a role extending beyond that of merely providing sufficient housing and managing it conventionally. One of the more interesting exponents of what has been termed a "Housing Plus" agenda is Respond!, a Christian housing association operating in the Republic of Ireland and highlighted at a consultation on the theme of Building for Community, organised by the Churches National Housing Coalition in 1996.

The work of Respond! is aimed at building vibrant, integrated, self-managed and self-reliant communities, rather than mere shelter or even simple, good standard accommodation. Respond! provides pre-tenancy and post-tenancy courses in estate management, child care, parenting and mediation work, to equip its tenants with the requisite skills to bring about such systems of self-management and community empowerment.

It is policy to ensure that, from design stage to occupation, each development will seek to foster a community environment in which each resident is invited and empowered to pay a full and active part in the creation of "community ownership".

Respond!, as a charitable organisation whose object is the elimination of poverty and the betterment of the poor, can justify its work in the provision of social housing only if, in parallel, it can also seek to put forward programmes to de-ghettoise the estates it builds. Such integration includes the provision of pre-schools available to all and staffed by local residents trained under the aegis of Respond!. It also attempts to break the choking impact of long-term unemployment on its estates by development training and job-creation programmes with the assistance of the National Training Agency (FAS). In 1995, Respond! employed 97 people under a Community Employment scheme. These people were recruited from, and based mainly in, its own estates across the country. Since its inception, some 10 people have managed to find full-time jobs through the scheme.

The conclusion of CNHC's consultation was that the churches still have a long way to go if they are to have a significant and lasting impact in this area. It stated: "It is only when the church is fully and actively present within situations and areas of greatest need, and where it is willing to commit resources to working on a long-term basis among the marginalised, that it has a contribution to make; and this is still a relatively rare phenomenon."

Yet, having surveyed the scene of housing and homelessness in Britain today, it is clear that the churches continue to have a major role to play in the task of bridging the divide between the unhoused, the badly housed and the well-housed. In many ways, the churches' record over the past 150 years and more in addressing homelessness and housing need is one of which they can rightly be proud.

Even today, in spite of diminished role and resources, the Church remains a significant provider of succour and an agent of change – not least through the voluntary efforts of thousands of individual church members, both seen and unseen. Yet the changing landscape of social division, poverty and housing need continues to demand strategic thinking and new kinds of response that go beyond mere amelioration.

The challenge to the Church is to seek new ways to deploy its unique and still powerful combination of assets – its community base, its historic resources of land and property, its huge pool of willing members and its political muscle – in the task of re-building community at the beginning of the third millennium.

Niall Cooper is national co-ordinator of Church Action on Poverty. He was formerly national organiser of the Churches National Housing Coalition.

Selected reading
Housing – a Moral Issue (Department of Social Responsibility, Catholic Bishops' Conference. 1985).
We Don't Choose to be Homeless – an Inquiry into Preventing Single Homelessness (CHAR. 1996).
Quarterly Homelessness Statistics (DETR. March 1998).
Anne Power and Rebecca Tunstall *Swimming Against the Tide: Progress or Polarisation on 20 Unpopular Estates*, (Rowntree Foundation. 1995).
The Price of Social Exclusion (National Federation of Housing Associations. 1995).
From Sympathy to Solidarity (London Churches Group. 1996).
Just Homes for All, It's Not Too Much to Ask (Churches National Housing Coalition, 1993).

Chapter Fourteen

Roads to reconciliation: The Church and crime

by Russell Webster

What has the Church got to do with crime? This might seem an odd question to ask, but throughout our history, the Church has been central to the development of the system for administrating criminal justice in this country. The roots of our criminal code lie in the Ten Commandments, and the role of the church in providing moral guidance has been central in encouraging observance of the law.

The great penal reforms of the Victorian era were led by Elizabeth Fry and others who were primarily motivated by their spiritual beliefs that there was something of God in everyone, including convicted criminals. This influence has continued into this century. The original probation officers were known as police court missionaries, and many of the charities set up to help and support prisoners and ex-offenders drew their inspiration from Christian beliefs.

Today, however, the criminal justice system attempts rehabilitation by "confronting offending behaviour", rather than by promoting spiritual reform. We no longer sentence prisoners to silent contemplation of the Bible, as we did in Victorian times. Bible study classes may abound in contemporary prisons, but it is hard for sceptics not to consider that, for many, attendance is more to do with getting out of the cell than a genuine search for redemption.

The Church no longer seeks to set the moral tone for the nation. Where preaching is broadcast on TV and radio, it is less frequently concerned with interpreting God's law and more likely to concentrate on relatively uncontentious and humanitarian aspirations, such as combating poverty in the Third World or showing consideration to our neighbours.

Increasingly, the Church has stepped aside from the debate on crime and punishment. Its public response to crime is becoming progressively secular. An incidence of this was the decision by the Sheffield diocese in early 1998 to ban a convicted paedophile from attending church services when children were present. This decision to adopt an approach that was more about managing risk than encouraging repentance received national publicity. The difficulty in enforcing the ban and the Diocese's statement that it would seek an injunction if the ban were broken only served to emphasise the bureaucratic approach.

However, it is arguable that there is a need for a moral and spiritual dimension in tackling crime and that churches are the obvious candidates to take on this role. Before examining a role for modern churches in tackling crime, it is important to define the "crime problem" and assess whether the secular response to offending is working.

The media presentation of crime is that society is more lawless than it has ever been and that shocking and heinous crimes are committed against children and old people on a regular basis. If we turn to the official figures, we find that it is certainly true that recorded crime has increased markedly over the last generation. A total of 1,666,000 notifiable offences were recorded by the police in 1971, while the peak year, 1993, saw 5,677,000 offences – an increase of over threefold in 22 years. Crime figures have stabilised and fallen slightly over the last few years, but even the slight fall may be connected to differences in recording practice and the stage of the economic cycle.

Again, if we examine the evidence of whether crime is becoming nastier, we find official statistics endorse this view. If we define nastier crime in the broad terms of violent and sexual offences, it is again true that this form of crime has increased. The average year on year increase of violent crime from 1987 to 1997 was 6.5 per cent; the average increase in the same time period for sexual offences was over 3 per cent. In the year ending June 1997, there were 33,000 sexual offences and 246,000 violent offences committed.

However, when we look more closely at the figures, we find that a large proportion of criminal offences are concentrated in the poorest areas of the country. Nearly half of all crimes take place in only a tenth of the neighbourhoods. Within these high crime areas we find that individuals and their households are often the victims of a large number of crimes. This phenomenon has been called "repeat victimisation" and the Home Office-funded Police Research Group has summarised a number of studies with the statement that "areas with high crime rates are disproportionately characterised by high rates of repeat victimisation".

In addition to this rise in crime, we also find considerable evidence in the media and in academic research of a great rise in the fear of crime. The Home Office has increasingly incorporated the investigation of fear of crime into its annual British Crime Surveys. A specific Home Office publication on this subject found that between 48 and 65 per cent of people were worried or very worried about being the victim of a burglary, rape or mugging; that 61 per cent of Asian people and 49 per cent of Black people were worried about being the victim of a racist attack; that inner-city residents were more fearful about crime; and that people in manual occupations were more fearful about crime.

The study, concluding that fear of crime itself may lead to the commission of more crime, stated: "It can lead to spirals of crime involving the abandonment of urban public space, disinvestment and the progressive segregation of the affluent and the poor in large cities."

Three factors in particular seem important in aggravating this fear of crime: party politics, the representation of crime in the media, and a feeling of powerless and over-reliance on the state to deal with all criminal activity. Crime and punishment seem always to have been highly politically charged issues. However, away from the soundbites and campaigning at election time, there was until recently considerable more consensus on the substance of most major criminal legislation than either main political party wished to admit. There was a good deal of backstage cross-party collaboration in supporting criminal justice legislation in the 1980s, and the legislation was generally evidence-based and well-drafted by civil servants. The most ambitious piece of legislation was the 1991 Criminal Justice Act, which sought to set a coherent framework for sentencing offenders in the UK. The aim was to sentence the relatively small proportion of offenders who had committed more serious crimes to longer prison sentences, with a clear period of supervision on release, and to supervise in the community the vast majority of those committing less serious property-related offences.

The Act was implemented in October 1992 and had a rapid

impact on judges and magistrates, with the number of offenders sentenced to imprisonment falling markedly. However, the following spring, two-year-old Jamie Bulger was killed by two children and the issue of young offenders became a political hot potato. Kenneth Clarke, the then Home Secretary, immediately ripped all the reforming powers out of the 1991 Act and there followed a blizzard of poorly thought-out legislation aimed more at short-term political gain than effective policy.

The Labour opposition fought on this ground. One of the most unedifying political spectacles of the year leading up to the 1997 general election was the battle between Michael Howard, the Home Secretary, and Jack Straw, his political "shadow" during that election and then his successor, to see who could be toughest on crime. This was a battle that the Church watched in silence from the sidelines.

Having established their respective rallying cries – "Prison Works" and "Tough on crime, tough on the causes of crime" – these two men traded blow for blow, covering almost every area of criminal activity, and drawing attention to some new ones along the way. New measures for released sex offenders were matched by zero tolerance of beggars and windscreen washers. The expansion of electronic tagging was confronted by a clampdown on nuisance neighbours. This political battle was fought so fiercely because crime was seen to be of increasing concern to the general public.

But there has also been the sensationalising of crime. Consider the effects of the media on fear of crime. In the judgment of newspaper editors, crime certainly seems to be of major public interest. From the shock-horror front pages featuring the most extreme and distressing offences in the tabloid press to *The Times* newspaper's serialisation of Gitta Sereny's book on the child killer Mary Bell, crime makes headline news.

Many of the leader comments in the press appear to stimulate and then support pressure for longer prison sentences – an apparent endorsement of Michael Howard's approach. However, recent Home Office research has revealed that the general public's perception of the over-leniency of the criminal justice system is largely inaccurate. Over half of those surveyed under-estimated the average length of sentence passed on rapists, muggers and burglars by 30 per cent or more. The research concluded that "people with lower levels of educational attainment, older people and those who read tabloid newspapers tended to have poorer knowledge of crime and criminal justice than others".

But there is a third factor linked with a fear of crime – an increasing feeling of powerlessness and a perception that only the state, in the form of the criminal justice system, can protect us. A number of commentators have commented on the growing preoccupation of many of us with risk and personal protection. There is an ongoing debate about how much we should protect our children from all risks and how much exposure to the real world is vital in equipping them to protect themselves as young adults.

David Faulkner of Oxford University has written eloquently on the consequence of this obsession with risk and an "exclusive" view of the world. He says: "Responsibility is placed firmly on criminals, either individually for the particular offences they have committed, or collectively as if they were a separate group who are outside normal or legitimate society. Unruly children, single parents, refugees, the mentally ill and social security claimants have also been described – or demonised – in this way. Dealing with crime and its consequences is seen as a matter for the police, the courts and other statutory services, not for society or communities, and the obvious and proper method is by detection and punishment. Deterrence and incapacitation by imprisonment are the most effective means of prevention, and an indefinite rise in the prison population – by 50 per cent in five years, with further increases projected, with its associated costs – can be accepted without serious question. Justice becomes a process to be accelerated and made more efficient and more effective in maximising its outputs, which are convictions and punishment."

This exclusive approach has been manifested frequently over the last year in public concern over the release of convicted sex offenders. Protests and the beginnings of vigilantism have resulted in driving dangerous paedophiles underground, where they cannot be monitored and supervised.

But this contemporary perception of crime in Britain, while it may be based on fact, is distorted and does not recognise that both the perpetrators and victims of crime are disproportionately concentrated within our most disadvantaged communities.

We have noted a feeling of powerlessness, of reliance on the criminal justice system and a wish for harsher punishment. Can the state protect us? To find the answer to this we need to examine the way in which the post-1997 government has sought to implement its manifesto promise to be "tough on crime, tough on the causes of crime". It has done this in two ways: by introducing new legislation and by improving the efficiency and co-ordination of the criminal justice system.

The major piece of legislation is the Crime and Disorder Act 1998, which extends the state's role in intervening not just in criminal activity but in anti-social behaviour too. A range of sentences will result in wide-ranging new powers, including imposing local curfews on all young people under 10 years old, banning named individuals from specific forms of anti-social behaviour, ordering parents to attend classes to improve their ability to control their children and bringing young children under 10 under the jurisdiction of the criminal justice system for the first time. It remains to be seen whether these initiatives will be successful in preventing offending, but in the short term they will certainly increase the number of people defined as criminals.

The legislation is being accompanied by a review of the working of the criminal justice system to increase effectiveness and collaboration. However laudable this aim, there will be negligible impact on overall crime levels in the short term, as the following statistics show. In 1993, police officers succeeded in clearing up only 25 per cent of all recorded offences (which represents only five per cent of all offences committed). Even a 20 per cent increase in efficiency would only see 30 per cent of all recorded offences cleared up (six per cent of all offences committed).

The probation service has been supervising an increasing number of offenders with smaller numbers of probation officers. In 1996, 7,300 probation officers supervised 115,000 offenders in the community. Probation staff complain that caseloads are high and bureaucracy and recording take up a disproportionate amount of time, leaving them with as little as half-an-hour per offender per week to try to stop them re-offending. The government made it clear that financial considerations meant that the probation service would receive more resources only if its workload continued to grow. A report by the Audit Commission found that, in some areas, youth justice workers spent only a tenth of their time working directly with young offenders.

At mid-1998/99, the prison service was holding an average of 61,100 prisoners on any given day, compared to a figure of 48,600 in 1989. This figure is the highest ever and is projected to be as high as 92,600 by 2005. Despite this huge increase, the Home Office calculates that there need to be 10,000 more prisoners to effect a decrease in the crime rate of one per cent.

As for being tough on the causes of crime, the new government's main initiatives in this area were the welfare to work scheme, the improvement of education and the work of the social exclusion unit, which aimed to tackle high-risk groups such as those expelled from school or living on sink estates. Educational attainment and employment are clearly related to offending in the research literature. However, even if these policies are successful they will take many years to bear fruit, especially when the scale of the problem is contemplated. An estimated 34 per cent of men born in 1953 had been convicted of a standard list offence (that is, not a motoring offence) by their 40th birthday.

Given this situation, it seems unlikely that the government can make a significant impact on crime levels in the short term. Indeed, there is a danger that, with the main emphases on more effective operation of the criminal justice system and preventative work, those who are currently engaged in a life of crime are likely to receive little help to encourage them to change. Similarly, there is little evidence that the typical short-term (normally a maximum of three years) community safety initiatives have had much impact on those neighbourhoods which are experiencing the most crime.

The foregoing suggests a picture in which crime has a growing negative impact on people's lives. Britain's poorest people are more likely to be victims of crime and more likely to have their quality of life affected by their fear of crime. They feel that the state is more lenient on criminals than it is, and they want to be protected. The criminal justice workers charged with this duty are doing their best but are unlikely to reduce the level of crime significantly in the short term. Most of these workers are professionals who commute into areas of deprivation to do their jobs and retire in the evening to safer suburbs.

A number of commentators – and indeed, to an extent, the

government – have argued for a more "inclusive" approach; the new Labour term was "stakeholder society". This approach has been characterised by a belief in the capacity and will of individuals to make positive changes if they are given opportunities and encouragement. The approach has emphasised rights and responsibilities on a community as well as an individual basis. So while the community has the right to expect certain standards of behaviour from its members, it has the responsibility to support its own vulnerable and disadvantaged members. Solutions to social problems generally are found by an inclusive approach based on community members – neighbours and parents – rather than relying on outside professionals. These solutions aim to give opportunities to those in trouble, to include them in a vision of the future rather than punish them for their actions and exclude them.

The problem with this viewpoint is that while it makes excellent copy in books and articles and good material for political speeches, the inclusive approach comes up short without anyone to lead it and drive it. There have been numerous neighbourhood initiatives that have made a positive impact on local problems in the short term. Too often these are the result of an injection of cash from a government scheme – City Challenge, Safer Cities, Single Regeneration Budgets – which appoints a co-ordinator who galvanises the local community for a short period of time before moving on when the funding runs out (normally after a maximum of three years).

Creating an inclusive society is a long-term project; it is a moral and spiritual enterprise, and one that needs to be led by individuals or organisations that are going to be around in the long term. Currently, there is a lack of leadership, involvement and participation among many of our poorest communities. The Church is ideally placed to start making a difference. It does not need to start out – like so many of the professional community empowerment (or "capacity building") organisations imported from the US – by writing a mission statement. The Church has always had a mission to embrace the poor and the vulnerable, to search for the lost sheep and bring them back into the fold. There is a real opportunity to put this mission into practice in modern Britain.

In recent years, much has been written about the "underclass" – people who feel marginalised and alienated from society, people for whom the concepts of "community" and "citizenship" have little meaning in their everyday lives. The Church's role is to reach out to these people, to include them in society and not allow them to be excluded and written off. In the current culture of protecting oneself from risk and condemning rather than understanding others, many offenders are seen as people to ignore and stay away from. In the past, it was hoped that young offenders would eventually sort themselves out, find jobs and partners, have children and settle down and "grow out of crime". The latest research exposes this as a myth.

So how can the Church reach out? Angela Sarkis, chief executive of the Church Urban Fund, has argued that there are three meeting points for communities in contemporary Britain: the school, the pub and the church. The church can have the most impact by changing the attitudes of local communities towards offenders. Leading by example, the church can preach the New Testament message of forgiveness to supplant the re-emergence of the Old Testament tenet of "an eye for an eye, a tooth for a tooth".

By working closely with local communities, local churches can unpick the stereotyping and demonisation of young offenders. While public opinion, as presented in the media, is characterised by growing intolerance of crime and hardline attitudes to punishment, there has been a worldwide growth in the mediation movement, sometimes known as "restorative justice".

Victim-Offender Mediation Programmes (VOMPs) bring offenders face-to-face with the victims of their crimes, with the assistance of a trained mediator, usually a community volunteer. Crime is personalised as offenders learn the human consequences of their actions, and victims (who are largely ignored by the justice system) have the opportunity to speak their minds and air their feelings to the one who most ought to hear them, contributing to the healing process of the victim.

Offenders take meaningful responsibility for their actions by mediating a restitution agreement with the victim, to restore the victim's losses in whatever ways that may be possible. Restitution may be monetary or symbolic; it may consist of work for the victim, community service or anything else that creates a sense of justice between the victim and the offender.

The VOMPs have been mediating meaningful justice between crime victims and offenders for over 20 years; there are now over 300 such programmes in the US and Canada, and about 500 in England, Germany, Scandinavia, Eastern Europe, Australia and New Zealand. Remarkably consistent statistics from a cross-section of the North American programmes show that about two-thirds of the cases referred resulted in a face-to-face mediation meeting; over 95 per cent of the cases mediated resulted in a written restitution agreement; and over 90 per cent of those restitution agreements are completed within one year. On the other hand, the actual rate of payment of court-ordered restitution (nationally) is typically only from 20-30 per cent.

This difference seems to be attributable to the fact that offenders seldom experience court-ordered restitution as a moral obligation. It seems like just one more fine being levied against them by an impersonal court system. When the restitution obligation is reached voluntarily and face-to-face, offenders experience it in a very different way. Perhaps most important, after facing the victims of their crimes, offenders commit fewer and less serious offences than similar offenders who are processed by the traditional juvenile or criminal justice system.

It is this moral dimension of the mediation process that makes it a natural area for the Church to become involved in. But, to establish its moral authority, the Church needs to be working with local communities at grass roots level and at a preventative as well as problem resolution level. Of course, some of this work is already going on and is the meat and drink of the pastoral duties of church workers from many faiths and denominations. However, sometimes there is a need to kick-start this work and give it a higher profile.

An interesting initiative was launched on the Pendower estate in Benwell, Newcastle upon Tyne, in 1998. The Church Urban Fund gave an £18,000 grant to set up a couple or family in a council house on this high-crime estate to provide a "good neighbour" service. The tenants will have a council house rent-free and will provide a room where they can entertain local residents and help them to solve their problems. The local vicar, the Rev. Richard Taylor, stated: "We want to find a family, or small group, who will move into the house and form a focus for the community. We want them to be good neighbours and set an example. The existence of a Good Neighbour House may make it easier for others to be good neighbours too. This could improve the general atmosphere of the estate. People have lost the knack of getting along together and feeling part of a community."

The challenge and opportunity for the Church is its potential to work within communities, to help local people raise their expectations in life and to feel that their communities, their families and they themselves are worth fighting for and protecting – and that the means to this protection is not to brand individuals as trouble-makers and drive them out, but to show them a better way and to encourage them to contribute.

The present government has been very keen on "joined-up solutions to joined-up problems". The Church has a crucial role to play in this "joining up", as a contributor with a great deal of experience and wisdom to offer about reaching out to those at greatest risk and for whom public sector provision has had limited effect. This role is one that the church should embrace if it wishes to regain the moral and spiritual influence it once had.

Russell Webster is an independent consultant specialising in partnership approaches to dealing with substance misuse and crime.

Selected Reading

Povey, Prime and Taylor *Notifiable Offences 1997* (Home Office Research and Statistics Directorate. 1998).

Anderson, Chenery and Pease *Biting back: Tackling Repeat Burglary and Car Crime* (Police Research Group, Crime Detection and Prevention Series; Paper 58. 1995).

M. Hough *Anxiety About Crime: Findings from the 1994 British Crime Survey* (Home Office Research Study 147, 1995).

Hough and Roberts *Attitudes to Punishment: Findings from the 1996 British Crime Survey* (Home Office 1998).

G. Barclay *The Criminal Justice System in England and Wales* (Home Office. 1995).

White and Powar *Revised Projection of Long-term Trends in the Prison Population to 2005* (Home Office Research and Statistics Directorate. 2/98).

Graham and Bowling *Young People and Crime* (Home Office Research Study 145. 1995).

Price *Can Mediation Produce Restorative Justice for Victims and Offenders?* (Victim Offender Reconciliation Program; website www.vorp.com).

Gathering together:
By way of conclusion

By Gerard Lemos and Giles Goddard

From the monastic institutions of the Middle Ages through to the poor laws the churches have given sustenance to the poor and succour to the sick, historically in rather minimal forms. In 1770 the vestry of St Mary's Newington in London churlishly complained that it was "burdened with numerous and expensive poor". At the end of the nineteenth century the rector of St Peter's, Walworth, emptied his crypt of interred bodies and the children of the adjoining school started having meals there. History has not recorded the children's views of the previous occupants of the crypt. A hundred years later the present rector hopes that the crypt can be rebuilt with state funding into a community centre of a rather higher grade.

The growth of the welfare state throughout the twentieth century, but particularly since the war, has usurped from the church the role of welfare provision. Without that role and with falling attendance, in most bars across the country the conversation has turned at one time or another: so what's left for the Church? The essays in this book are a series of eloquent, heartfelt ripostes. The churches' roles in the community are mutable and manifold. Little wonder really, given that the rituals, beliefs and values of our society are also now manifold and mutable.

This transformation in role has certainly brought an unwelcome marginalisation for the Church, but also liberation – a freedom to innovate. This freedom is an opportunity for institutions in which innovation has not kept pace with social change. Much that is truly innovatory, for the community and for the church, is recounted here – challenges to homelessness and to the treatment of asylum seekers, the inclusion of people on the margins, in schools, in health care and much else besides.

In Britain, America and Japan in the nineteenth century religion played a powerful part in 'renorming' as well as reforming society for an industrial age that, to begin with, had few qualities of civilisation. The battle against alcoholism, gambling, slavery, delinquency, prostitution and child labour, to name only the most pernicious depredations, were fought more vigorously and rigorously from the pulpit than from the despatch box. All denominations were engaged in building a dense network of charities and voluntary organisations, many of which despite the growth of the welfare state, still grow and thrive in that huge space between the family and the state - civil society. Indeed, as we begin to reform the welfare state, many of the older religious-based charities look set to play an unprecedented role in, for example, the care of children, older people and people with disabilities. The wheel is turning once more, if not towards the church, than decisively towards organisations that owe their initiation to religion.

But the social purpose has not superseded the parish ministry or its equivalents in other denominations. The churches cling tenaciously to the view that a human representative and a building of the church should be present everywhere that calls itself a community. The community described in this book is one that links people in a place to people dispossessed, both in their midst and elsewhere. The link here is between a sense of place, say in Bromley-by-Bow. A wider moral purpose feeds the wish to do something for people in need right here. Unifying place, morality and spirituality has been the church's historic mission, but it may not be equal to the task facing us.

Some religious conservatives hope and many liberals fear that the response to the upheaval underway will be a wholesale return to orthodoxy, perhaps of the fundamentalist stripe, not just in Islam, but in Christianity and Judaism too. But in a society as culturally diverse as ours, whose orthodoxy would prevail? Many ephemeral 'orthodoxies' will flourish reflecting people, places, histories and cultures. Community feeling is unlikely to arise out of a universal adherence to a single set of revealed beliefs.

Another revolution, comparable in scale and consequences to the great Industrial Revolution, is underway - globalisation, the Internet, biotechnology are all interplaying with one another to deliver us into what the influential American sociologist, Manuel Castells, has called the network society. In the network society there will be network communities. Communities of work, of interest and of identity will not take over from communities of place, but they will certainly have an independent life of their own which will not be defined by place.

Along with the space of place, new spaces have been formed. The Internet is one, as described in one of the essays here. It is becoming a network of virtual communities of interests, identity and place.

And in these spaces questions of morality have certainly arisen. Criminal gangs are trading vast sums of money on the Internet. People use the Internet for sex more than for any other reason. From the other moral perspective, revolution in Mexico has been promoted on the Internet, as have been attempts to stop genetically modified farming and to overthrow capitalism in European capitals. Unlikely as it seems now, these 'virtual activists' may, much mutated, come to be seen as the suffragettes and abolitionists of our times. Virtual moral discourses are being enacted. In that case, should there not be ministers for the 'parishes' of interest on the Internet? And overarching them, there is an inexorable logic to seeing the Net as a whole as a diocese - of course, eventually with a bishop of its own. If the existing churches do not respond, new ones will; of that we may be sure.

The absence of fixed beliefs is what is leading to the search for a humane value system, not just on the old questions of the poor who are still with us, but also the new questions of diversity and identity, of technology, of genetics. The new ethics will have to challenge unfairness against some of the groups towards which many churches continue to maintain a powerful antipathy, notably lesbians and gay men. For lesbians and gay men are another sort of 'virtual community', linked by identity, not by place or by technology. And there are plenty more like them - environmentalists, animal liberationists, new age travellers. All of these new social movements have developed a morality, and in the case of new age groups, new forms of ritual and worship alongside their identities. These debates could be carried on independent of the churches and some would be sanguine about that prospect. The title of Bishop Richard Holloway's book, the spiritual leader of 50,000 non-virtual Scottish Episcopalians, argues this case, *Godless Morality: Keeping religion out of ethics*. He says,

> "Just because the connection between ethics and religion
> has been broken, it does not follow that it is no longer
> possible to have ethics. It may mean we have to discover
> and promote the importance of a non-religious ethic. And
> such an ethic could be a genuinely ecumenical ethic that

appealed in its broad principles to people who are religious
and to people without religion, to people who believed in
God and to people who did not."

Fusing joint ethics from pick and mix religions may prove
complicated. Many a priest was rendered speechless with
astonishment by the utterances of the former England football
manager, Glenn Hoddle. His pick and mix faith was certainly
self-serving, but his convictions are deeply held and create in
his mind a coherent moral code, leading him to feel indignant
that his views on people with disabilities were unfairly
misrepresented.

But even if the moral dimension of the churches work can
be re-invented, the role of churches and faith communities in
making and re-making sacred rituals will still be up for grabs.
Customs are being borrowed, shared and updated. Rituals are
being fused. Many of the organised religions look on in horror
at lesbian and gay marriages. If we are to have ministers for
communities on the Internet, we shall certainly have to have
chaplains to the lesbian and gay communities, people with
disabilities and all the rest. In the longer term, it will not be
possible to restrict the discussion to the relatively narrow
question of who can be ordained.

Francis Fukuyama has announced in his book, *The Great
Disruption*, the continuation of religion, some of it of the Hoddle
sort, after the end of history,

> "People will turn to religious tradition not because they
> accept the truth of revelation, but precisely because the
> absence of community and the transience of social ties in
> the secular world make them hungry for ritual and cultural
> tradition. They will help the poor or their neighbours not
> because the doctrine tells them they must, but because
> they want to serve their communities and find that faith-
> based organisations are the most effective ways of doing so.
> They will repeat ancient prayers and re-enact old rituals
> not because they believe they were handed down by God,
> but rather because they want their children to have the
> proper values and want to enjoy the comfort of ritual and
> the sense of shared experience it brings."

Fukuyama may turn out to be a false prophet. Bishop

177

Holloway may be right: ethics will be divorced from religion as social welfare has been. We are certainly entering a multi-faith century, just as we are leaving one, but civil society and community feeling remains along with the role of the faith communities in inventing and re-inventing them and the rituals that surround them. Balancing innovation and tradition, ever in perpetual Newtonian motion, is a task that, in a good society, can never be neglected. Chaos would ensue. The contributors to this volume and the people with whom they work are engaged in striking this balance.

Gerard Lemos is the co-author with Michael Young (Lord Young of Dartington) of *The Communities We Have Lost and Can Regain*.

The **Rev. Giles Goddard** is rector of St Peter's, Walworth in London.

Index